STRONG
Enough

CHOOSING COURAGE, RESILIENCE, AND TRIUMPH

ANNE GRADY

Graphic Design by Brenda Hawkes

Edited by Phyllis Jask

Author photos by Kathy Whittaker Photography

Printed in the United States of America

ISBN-13: 978-1541332713

ISBN-10: 1541332717

DEDICATIONS

To anyone who has ever questioned their courage, strength, and resolve. You are not alone, and you are Strong Enough.

And to my family. I love you with all of my heart. Thank you for teaching me that I am Strong Enough.

PRAISE FOR *STRONG ENOUGH*

"She may deny it, but Anne is a true inspiration, and her latest book is a revelation. With liberal doses of compassion and humor, she offers valuable insights as to why we get stuck in undesirable situations and how to find the courage to step out of our comfort zone and consciously make a change for the better. Anne's unflinchingly honest account of how she has personally overcome what is more than anyone's fair share of challenges lends an authenticity to the lessons she shares and makes for a compelling read that will stay with you long after the last page."

—Ann Dahlquist, Fortune 500 Company

"Study after study over the last 20 years has caused science to conclude that everything for a human being depends on mindset. How long and how well we live all depends on our state of mind. A chronically worried, stressful, and pessimistic mindset thwarts our success and can eventually kill us, while a dynamically positive and peaceful mindset can literally heal our body, raise our intelligence, and amplify the higher brain function that enables us to succeed. That's why a book like *Strong Enough* is so important. It offers you the path to a change of mind that changes everything."

—Don Joseph Goewey, author of *The End of Stress: Four Steps to Rewire Your Brain*

"Life isn't complicated, but it can be challenging, as Anne Grady's personal story so powerfully illustrates. Anne simplifies coping. She teaches you how to stand up, be strong, and remain resilient. Anne's inspiration for and embodiment of quiet courage certainly makes a deafening roar."

—Rhonda Duffy, founder DuffyRealtyofAtlanta.com

"A refreshing approach to finding strength within ourselves, while rising above personal/life struggles. Anne's ability to connect with readers through her own "strength-finding journey," not only creates a space for self-reflection, but also the necessary push to MOVE and do something about it. Anne is a true reminder that obstacles don't have to be life-threatening, but rather life-building."

—Gina Grandone, Fortune 500 Company

"In a funk? World treating you like a punching bag? Plagued with self-doubt? Anne helps you mine your courage and get to the other side. Her tough life experiences demonstrate that anyone can step into her strength and emerge feeling like a badass."

   —Lisa Cummings, CEO, Lead Through Strengths

"Anne Grady's story is not only hard-hitting—it is heart-hitting. This is a transformative book that takes a fresh approach to life's hard knocks using Anne's trademark ingredients of guts, grit, and humor. If you've ever doubted yourself or your ability to overcome the most devastating obstacles life throws at you, this book and this speaker will raise you up, help you soften your hard edges, and leave you feeling like Rocky Balboa. It is a masterpiece."

   —Anne Bruce, bestselling author of *Discover True North, Be Your Own Mentor,* and
      Speak for a Living

"You're more than you think you are and this book proves it. In it, Anne Grady details her own life's struggles with her mentally ill child while at the same time discovering a tumor and breaking her foot in four places. These challenges forced Anne to realize she has deep reserves of strength and empowerment. And now we all get to benefit from it."

   —Dr. Matt James, Integrative Health expert and author of *Ho`oponopono*

"Anne Grady has offered us a truly special and powerfully encouraging guide that is both straightforward and richly complex. The guidance and wisdom is easy to follow, but it is well framed by the brave personal stories that are touching, challenging, and important."

   —Jonathan Ellerby PhD, bestselling author of *Inspiration Deficit Disorder*

"This book spoke to me with relatable subject matter and actionable suggestions. I took the initiative to establish a goal and I feel stronger and more resilient. I have already begun my actions to become a stronger me!"

   —Alicia Davis, Director at DELL

"An idea is a creative life force, a living dynamic organism. All successful people learn to use their gut instinct to cope with discomfort and use it as a catalyst for growth. This book gives us the formula to minimize the expectation of perfection and learn to dance—with gratitude— with what we unconsciously create in our lives."

   —Suzy Batiz, founder of Poopourri.com and serial entrepreneur

CONTENTS

ACKNOWLEDGMENTS

To all the people in my life, and even those I do not know personally, many of you have inspired me to speak and write for a living. I want you to know that I am incredibly grateful.

It is from my journey to find courage that I have found my brave heart. It is from seeking more resilience in my life that I have found ways to accomplish more than I ever thought possible. It is from my never-ending quest to triumph over scarcity, depression, mediocrity, and perfectionism that I have found the ability to let go and play an important role for my family, friends, business associates, readers, and communities when they've needed me the most.

At the end of the day, it comes down to holding on tight to my inner strength and courage, facing my vulnerabilities and fears, accepting joy and happiness because I deserve it, and expressing gratitude every chance that I get.

I hope this book allows you to do the same.

INTRODUCTION

I was walking out of the house for an early meeting. I was being interviewed for a blog article, and I was running late. Seconds before I walked out the door, Evan, my then-12-year-old son, had a volcanic meltdown. He had started to make a lot of progress, and his aggressive episodes were getting fewer and farther between. Until that morning. I don't even remember what set him off. My husband Jay had to hold Evan while he scratched, bit, and flailed around. After almost an hour of tears, picking up things that had been thrown, trying to fix furniture that had been broken, and cleaning up parts of my house that had been destroyed, I was exhausted. I called the interviewer and rescheduled. I certainly didn't feel like being chipper for an interview. All I wanted to do was cry.

Thankfully, she was very understanding. We met a week later at a local Starbucks.[1] Some of the questions were the typical "Tell me about your life" variety, but some were questions I had never been asked: "What is the best gift you've ever given?" "What book should be required reading for all human beings?" "How did you make your first buck?" "Who is your celebrity doppelgänger?" Her last question, though, really made me stop and think. She asked, "If you had 30 seconds to make a speech to the world, what would your message be?"

I felt incredible pressure to come up with something profound, but nothing profound came to mind. Instead, I shared one of the

---

1 Anne Grady, interview by Melissa Lombard, "Cup 117: Anne Grady—Communication Expert, Curveball Dodger and Cake Lover," *Coffee with a Stranger*, available at http://www.melissalombard.com/cup-117-anne-grady-communication-expert-curveball-dodger-and-cake-lover.

biggest lessons I've learned in my journey of raising two children, one with mental illness. I said, "You find what you look for. Stop looking for all the reasons life isn't fair and horrible things happen. Start looking for the right things, and you're more likely to find them. Don't be a victim. It's easy to blame everybody and everything around you for the things that aren't right in your life. It's another thing to say, 'Here's where I am. Here's what I have to work with. Let's make it move in the right direction.'"

Then without giving it an inch of thought, I blurted out, "Basically, *get off your ass and be grateful!*"

Truth is, that one sentence basically sums up my life philosophy. I have a habit of being pretty blunt. When I'm on stage, I'm no different. I lack the "filter" most professional speakers have, and I tell it like it is. I don't sugar coat my life or make it sound glamorous. For example, just now while typing this paragraph, I was called to unclog a toilet. Not so glamorous!

I have felt conflicted, wondering if Evan's story was mine to tell. As he has gotten older, he has asked me to share his story as a way to help others know they are not alone. He understands the shame and stigma attached to mental illness first hand, and his bravery and courage in allowing me to share his story is one of my proudest accomplishments.

It has been a bumpy road, and I have learned some incredibly valuable lessons about being grateful, resilient, courageous, and triumphant. I wish I could tell you I've learned these lessons while enjoying a spa day or in the classroom, but the truth is, I've been through the ringer.

My first book, *52 Strategies for Life, Love & Work: Transforming Your Life One Week at a Time,* was my survival guide, and I published it during the most tumultuous year of my life. It is a collection of strategies that I used to strengthen relationships, achieve personal and professional goals, and maintain my sanity—or what little I had left. This book, however, is about discovering what strong enough means to you…strong enough to choose courage even when you're terrified of the outcome, strong enough to be resilient when you have been knocked down, and strong enough to master and claim triumph over whatever life throws your way.

It is important to understand that just like happiness, triumph comes in the little moments. No one feels triumphant all of the time. It is my hope that this book will inspire you to pay attention to those moments and to face every day with a resolve you may not even realize you have.

I will help you by challenging you to work through your own pain, your own struggles, and your own roadblocks with interactive activities and lessons. It is my hope that these lessons help you find your courage and resilience, and show you that you are strong enough.

MY LONG AND WINDING ROAD

Raising a mentally ill child is enough to make you crazy. It causes you to doubt everything you once knew about yourself. I've questioned myself as a mother, caregiver, spouse, friend, and as a person. It's like having an out-of-body experience every day—I see myself getting frustrated quickly and then I easily become overwhelmed with worry and anxiety. The more out of control I feel, the more I feel the need to control. I start to feel bad about the one role I'm supposed to be great at. Being a parent is my most important job. At least when you're unhappy in a job, you have the choice to leave it; however, leaving *this* job was never an option for me.

When Evan was an infant, I noticed something about him was different. As he grew, his behavior became increasingly unmanageable. I was a single mom, parenting all alone, and I thought I was absolutely losing it because those around me—doctors, friends, specialists, and practically everyone else—doubted that something was really wrong. And their doubt made me doubt myself: "If I were just more consistent…

If I were just a better disciplinarian… I was making mountains out of molehills and clearly exaggerating what we were going through…" Only I wasn't. Not only was I struggling to raise a child who was constantly irritable, aggressive, and angry, I was trying to convince other people I wasn't making it up. Finally, after visiting dozens of doctors, therapists, nutritionists, and everyone in between, Evan was diagnosed and people finally started to believe me. Although it took years to get an accurate diagnosis, the gist is a severe mood disorder, ADHD and incredible impulsivity, oppositional defiant disorder, and a neurological condition that created a "sunburn" on his brain. Have you ever had a bad sunburn, and when you rub against something it just irritates and hurts your skin? That's what Evan's brain is like. The littlest things can irritate him and set him off, and let me tell you, hell hath no fury like a child with mental illness.

Don't get me wrong. Every waking moment in my life is not filled with heartbreak. I laugh and have plenty of wonderful times with my family. Evan's mental illness often gives us perspective and unifies us in ways I never imagined. I see my daughter Rylee show empathy and forgiveness beyond the capacity of the typical teenager. When I married her dad (my husband Jay), she had her destiny decided for her, yet she took it all in stride. I'm proud to call her my own daughter. I am beyond blessed to have wonderful times with both of the kids. Evan can be loving, witty, and sweet. He has a good heart, and I am reminded every day how hard it must be for him to manage all of the emotions he struggles to control. It is from joyful times with my family that I draw my strength and find moments of triumph when I'm feeling downtrodden or lost.

The Discovery

Evan was first hospitalized in 2010. For two months, Jay and I lived at the Ronald McDonald House while Evan underwent inpatient psychiatric treatment. It was a humbling experience for all of us. Evan made progress, but his behavior was still a daily challenge. When we checked Evan into the hospital the second time, it was just as painful as the first. Probably even more so. The problems he was having clearly weren't getting better. With this on my mind, I had to fly to Iowa the next morning to deliver a speech. I had a raging migraine and was more stressed than I could ever remember being. I found a chair massage place at the airport and paid an exorbitant amount of money for some relief. I really tried to keep it together, but while getting massaged, I started to cry—uncontrollably. Actually, I sobbed the kind of sob that makes snot bubbles. Sorry for the graphic image, but it was one of *those* cries. The massage therapist was incredible. She shared with me that she had a special needs child as well, and we had an instant connection. She told me to call her when I got back to Austin for a 90-minute massage at my house—her treat! I couldn't pass that up!

While massaging my neck, she pointed out a lump behind my right ear. After feeling it, we were both convinced it was a swollen lymph node, but she suggested I get it checked out by a doctor. A few weeks passed and the lump wasn't going away. I saw a doctor and was prescribed antibiotics. They didn't work. The doctor suggested I see an ear, nose, and throat specialist, who ordered a CT scan.

I had a tumor in my salivary gland. The surgeon shared this news with us while we were discharging Evan from the hospital. *Are you f*&%@ng kidding me?* What should have been a joyful day just went down the toilet.

Surgery

On the day of my surgery, right before they administered that magical sleeping drug, I recorded a video. I smiled and told the kids how much I loved them and that everything was going to be fine. I would be done with surgery in a couple of hours, and I would be back to myself in no time.

Six hours into my surgery, the doctor went into the waiting room and asked my mom and Jay to have a seat. No good news ever starts with "have a seat." He said the tumor was much larger than he anticipated (the size of a small avocado), and because of its aggressive nature, I would have to have radiation to ensure that it didn't come back. He further explained that due to the size of the tumor, my facial nerve had stretched so far that the right side of my face was now completely paralyzed. Although he did his best to save the nerve, he wasn't sure if it would recover. I woke up the next day, and it was as if I'd had a stroke. I couldn't smile, blink, or close my right eye, and I now had a speech impediment. For anyone this would not be a good thing; for me as a professional speaker, I saw my career nosedive.

Surgery, the Sequel

Two days after the surgery, a small speck of dust scratched my cornea. That was more painful than recovering from surgery. I had to tape my eye closed, and it felt like glass shards were slicing my eyeball. I had to see yet another specialist because my eye couldn't close due to the paralysis, and we didn't know if or when my facial nerve would heal. The doctor told me I needed a gold weight implanted into my upper lid and my lower lid stitched to hold it up.

I had to have eye surgery before undergoing radiation, but I needed to plan it around my speaking engagements. I was scheduled to go to India for a five-day speaking engagement in the summer, and I was determined to go. I was told to cancel the trip because radiation would take its toll, and I wouldn't be able to work.

It was now April and the week before both my birthday and my eye surgery. My mom offered to watch the kids while Jay and I took the weekend off. We decided that since we had been so lucky lately (insert sarcasm here), we should go to Las Vegas. My eye still wouldn't close, so

I had to wear an eye patch. Half of my face was smiling (the other half always looked ticked off). I looked like a pirate.

Luck Be a Lady Tonight

We were in Las Vegas, and for the first time in a long time, I felt really good. Jay and I walked to Caesars Palace, and while walking down the stairs I turned to him and said, "For the first time since the surgery, I feel human again. I'm finally starting to feel better." As I uttered the last word, I fell down the stairs. The eye patch made depth perception difficult, and I completely missed a step. I didn't know whether to laugh or to cry. I did both.

I limped around for the next two days in complete agony. Jay urged me to get an x-ray, but I wasn't about to waste my precious kid-free Vegas time with a doctor. We flew back to Austin, and as soon as we got off the plane, I got an x-ray. My foot was broken in four places.

The next day was my eye surgery. I was in a giant boot, had half a face, and a giant gauze bandage covered my right eye. I was quite a sight. The day after the eye surgery was my birthday. Although I looked and felt completely pitiful, I was determined to have a good birthday. Jay had bought tickets months before to see one of my favorite stand-up comedians. The irony that we were going to see a comedy while in the midst of such tragedy was not lost on me.

From Radiation to Radiant

My radiation started in late April and for six weeks I had daily treatments. It was one of the most grueling things I've ever done. I was fitted with a giant face mask that was clamped to a table so I couldn't move. I looked like a storm trooper from *Star Wars*. Even though that was incredibly scary and uncomfortable, the worst part was the waiting room. Sometimes it took five minutes to be seen, but if it was a busy day, I could sit there for two hours before receiving my treatment. Do you know how many sick, dying people you see in a radiology waiting room? Too many. Painful as it was to see so many seriously ill people, I quickly saw my priorities come into focus (even with my one working eye). I met so many brave people, listened to their stories, and marveled at the strength they demonstrated.

Radiation was taking its toll and I was tired, but I was surprised at how well my body handled it. Around the first week of June, my radiologist noticed that my face looked, well, less droopy. I dismissed it and thought he was just trying to lift my spirits. That night, when I smiled (with the left side of my face), Jay said he saw a tooth on the right side. Until that moment, he could only see the teeth on the left. As days went by, he was able to count more teeth, and we realized that my smile was coming back. A week or so later, I was able to close my eye and blink. I was ecstatic! Not only was I able to go to India for the speaking engagement, but I was able to go with my face close to normal! The passport photo I had taken before the trip showed my facial paralysis. It was incredible to see the transformation from just weeks earlier. Over the course of the next several months, my face completely healed. Scans revealed that the tumor was gone. Hallelujah!

THE LESSONS I'VE LEARNED

As I write this book, it's strange to think back on everything that happened almost three years ago. On the one hand, it seems like an eternity has passed. On the other hand, it feels like yesterday.

I've shared this story during training and speaking events, and people asked how I was so brave. They said I was strong and inspirational. None of those things made sense to me. I didn't feel strong or brave, and I certainly didn't feel like an inspiration.

But something funny happened. The more I shared my story and the more people thanked me for my message, the stronger I felt. The more others got inspired, the more inspired I became. I realized that I had been courageous and strong, not because I wasn't afraid, but because I was afraid and pushed through anyway. I began to appreciate my resilience and have even practiced it a few times since then. And if I had to go through hell and back, the least I could do was learn a lesson or two along the way and share what I've learned with others. Finding meaning in difficult situations is a courage and resilience exercise in itself. If I can help even one person find strength and courage, then everything I have gone through has meaning.

I was able to not only survive but thrive over the last 15 years solely on a combination of courage and resilience. Both are necessary, and neither can work alone. The combination is a winning formula:

Courage + Resilience = Triumph

Life is about the journey—and being strong enough to find the courage and resilience to face all that it places in our paths along the way. When we practice courage and resilience, we will triumph.

PART 1:
COURAGE

As I type this, Jay and I just finished a 90-minute, knock-down, drag out fight with Evan, who is now 13 years old. Jay had to restrain him after he started breaking things and throwing anything he could find. Jay has a bite mark on each arm and scratches to match, our kitchen looks like a war zone, and I look like I was on a bender all night—and it all happened before 8:00 am.

One of the benefits of having a child in special education is having the bus pick Evan up in our driveway. Unfortunately, this morning we had to send the bus to school without Evan on it. He was in a rage, and he was dangerous. After calming him (no small feat), getting him in the car, driving him to school, and debriefing his teachers, I am exhausted.

Now, here's how I define courage. Courage is getting him to school, talking to his teachers even though I just wanted to cry, coming back to the house, hugging Jay, laughing about our crazy life, and getting back to work. Courage is forgiving myself for the guilt that makes me question what I could have done differently. Courage is knowing he's going to come home after school and will act like nothing ever happened, because in his mind, it is over and he has moved on. Courage is hugging him tight and loving him anyway. And courage is tucking him in tonight, knowing it could start all over again in a few hours.

A GOOD TRACK RECORD

On really bad days, when I think I can't possibly make it through another hour, or I feel like I'm suffocating, I remind myself of one thing: so far my track record for making it through really bad days is 100 percent. Those are pretty good odds. If you think about it, you have a perfect track record as well. You have survived every obstacle you've encountered.

I've learned the critical importance of self-assurance. It's therapy, it's a life tool, and it saves me from losing my mind at times.

I am not the first person to declare such a feat. However, it took each and every one of my bad days to bring me to the place where I stand today. The trajectory of my journey has landed me in the place I am supposed to be—right here, right now. You can't control the cards you are dealt, only how you play them. But what happens if you're dealt really crappy cards?

Accepting your trajectory is sometimes the hardest thing to do. But I'm learning, and I'm doing it. And so can you. Notice I didn't say "I've learned it." This is not a one-and-done kind of lesson. This is a practice. It is a conscious choice that you have to make every day. And some days will be easier than others.

How do I get back up? I give myself permission to cry and grieve. I allow myself some time to mope, beg God, and feel scared. I take deep breaths and remind myself that I am strong enough to handle this.

Sometimes, I slip and let myself get really down. The real courage is being strong enough to celebrate the times I get it right, instead of beating myself up for the times I don't.

"Strength does not come from physical capacity. It comes from an indomitable will."

—Mahatma Gandhi

What Is Courage?

Courage is defined as *the ability to do something that you know is difficult or dangerous; mental or moral strength to persevere and withstand danger, fear, or difficulty.*[2]

I love the word *courage*. It means I have to make the decision every day to do something that I know will be difficult, and may even be dangerous. And I need all of the mental and moral strength I can muster to persevere.

Some days, I view courage as the sheer strength to pull myself out of bed and face the day. Other days it's having clear boundaries and

---

[2] Merriam-Webster's Collegiate Dictionary, 11th ed., s.v. "courage."

standing my ground when it would be easier to give in. Hell, trying on a bathing suit is a total act of courage.

There have been so many times when I've felt like I have lost my courage. I've come to realize that while we might lose sight of our courage, we haven't really lost it at all.

Flex Your Courage Muscles

How do you identify with the word *courage*? Do you associate it with a specific behavior or a mannerism? A characteristic? An emotion? A discipline? A virtue?

_____

_____

_____

_____

_____

_____

What does the word courage "look like" to you? How would you define it? What images come to mind? Take a second to write them down or even sketch them out.

_____

_____

_____

_____

_____

_____

Continued on the next page.

Flex Your Courage Muscles *Continued from the previous page.*

I see courage as an acronym with each letter having a meaning and definition that I can apply to my life.

C.O.U.R.A.G.E.

C = Compassion for yourself and others, even when you're exhausted

O = Overcoming fear and self-doubt

U = Understanding and tapping into your strengths

R = Recognizing all you have accomplished

A = Adapting and being flexible

G = Growing and learning

E = Enduring tough times

"Life shrinks or expands in proportion to one's courage." —Anaïs Nin

COURAGE COMES IN ALL SHAPES AND SIZES

Courage Is Relative

When I speak or teach a class, inevitably someone will approach me on a break or after the presentation and share his or her story. Their child, grandchild, niece, nephew, or neighborhood friend has a situation similar to mine. What's interesting is that nine times out of 10, they start with, "My situation is nothing compared to yours, but…." This is called *comparative suffering.*

Don't compare your pain and fear to the experiences of others. We all struggle at 100 percent. You are experiencing what you are experiencing, and if you're sharing it in the context I'm referring to, it probably sucks. Courage is relative to the person and the situation. What is scary to one person may be exhilarating to the next. I know people who are fearless when it comes to travel or sports, but they refuse to fall in love because they may get hurt.

Types of Courage

There is no one-size-fits-all when it comes to courage. We see things differently, and we experience different types of courage. None are better or worse than any other.

Intuitive Courage

- Questioning purpose and meaning.
- Reaching out to help others or to challenge injustice.
- Making time to meditate, be silent, and seek peace of mind.

Creative Courage

- Seeking self-expression.
- Transforming bold ideas into reality.
- Going with the flow.

Physical Courage

- Embracing bravery at the risk of bodily harm.
- Building physical strength, resilience, and awareness.
- Committing to discipline and training.

Moral Courage

- Doing the right thing despite the consequences.
- Matching words and actions with principles.
- Standing up for those who can't stand up for themselves.

Emotional Courage

- Being open to positive and negative emotions.
- Asking for forgiveness and forgiving others.
- Seeking help, feedback, guidance, coaching, or therapy.

Intellectual Courage

- Questioning your thinking and risking making mistakes.
- Discerning and telling the truth.
- Dealing with problems or difficult situations.

Social Courage

- Being comfortable in your own skin even at the risk of social disapproval.
- Expressing opinions respectfully, even if unpopular.
- Becoming involved with charities or social causes.

Flex Your Courage Muscles

Which types of courage come easily for you?

_____

_____

_____

_____

_____

Which are more difficult?

_____

_____

_____

_____

_____

COURAGE SELF-ASSESSMENT

Part of building courage is the willingness to self-assess, to really look at your thoughts and behaviors, and to identify your strengths and weaknesses. Take this self-assessment to see how you identify with courage.

Circle the following for each statement:

4 = Always   3 = Sometimes   2 = Rarely   1 = Never

1.	I make an effort to get out of my comfort zone.	4	3	2	1
2.	I deal with problems head on.	4	3	2	1
3.	I stand up for what I believe in.	4	3	2	1
4.	I believe calculated risks pay off.	4	3	2	1
5.	I respond well in crisis.	4	3	2	1
6.	I acknowledge my mistakes and move on.	4	3	2	1
7.	I respect and care for myself.	4	3	2	1
8.	I allow myself to be vulnerable.	4	3	2	1
9.	I believe courage can be developed.	4	3	2	1
10.	I speak up even when my viewpoint is unpopular.	4	3	2	1
11.	I admit when I am wrong.	4	3	2	1
12.	I am willing to change my behavior to get different results.	4	3	2	1
13.	I take action when it is needed.	4	3	2	1
14.	I face my fears.	4	3	2	1
15.	I use my voice to make an impact.	4	3	2	1
16.	I learn from challenging situations.	4	3	2	1
17.	I regularly set goals and challenge myself.	4	3	2	1
18.	I treat myself with kindness.	4	3	2	1
19.	I view failure as a learning opportunity.	4	3	2	1
20.	I am aware of what triggers my insecurity and self-doubt.	4	3	2	1

Scoring:

70–80 points = You are a courage warrior. Keep it up! Appreciate your strength and courage and take time to teach others how to do the same.

60–69 points = Continue to challenge yourself and embrace opportunities to grow your courage.

50–59 points = You have an opportunity to do something TODAY to grow your courage.
Fewer than 50 points = You are being too hard on yourself. Give yourself a break.

Flex Your Courage Muscles

The objective of this self-assessment is to help you identify what I call your "courage blockers." Everyone has them. Until you sit down and really go through the things you gravitate toward or run away from, it's difficult to know what's getting in the way or holding you back. I've found this easy-to-complete assessment helps keep me on track and alerts me to some of the barriers or limitations I'm creating.

Describe your strongest courage blockers. Pick one and set a goal.

_____

_____

_____

_____

_____

_____

What can you do this week to make subtle improvements? What action can you take today to overcome one of your blockers?

_____

_____

_____

_____

_____

_____

"Courage isn't having the strength to go on—
it is going on when you don't have strength."

—Napoleon Bonaparte

WHAT ARE YOUR COURAGE TRIGGERS?

No matter how courageous a person you are or how much confidence you have or have gained through personal experience, there usually comes a time when you feel you have lost your courage and your strength, or at least temporarily misplaced it.

If you pay attention, you will notice a pattern. There is usually something or someone that triggers a lack of self-esteem and confidence. For me, I've noticed that as I start to get frustrated and lose my cool with Evan, I start behaving in ways that make me feel bad about myself. I snap or get frustrated easily, I become controlling, and I feel my shoulders tighten. I've learned that when I feel these things, I have been triggered. My courage hasn't left me and my strength isn't gone, but I have to work twice as hard to hold on to them.

When you are triggered, the emotional part of your brain takes over. You are flooded with adrenaline, nor-adrenaline, cortisol, and testosterone. The same chemicals that were meant to protect you (freeze, fight, or flight), cause your logical brain to shut down. You lose the ability to solve problems, make decisions, and think rationally. When this happens, you have been emotionally hijacked, and it is difficult to see things as they really are. You go into protection mode, and until the perceived threat or trigger has gone, you will remain there.

Here are a few examples of triggers:

- Work
- Children
- Finances
- Relationships
- Illness
- Stress
- Overcommitting
- Loneliness
- Family dynamics
- Work/life balance
- Uncertainty

Once you are aware of your triggers, you can manage how you choose to react to them.

Flex Your Courage Muscles

What typically triggers you? Where are you? Who is involved?

_____

_____

_____

_____

What action can you take to proactively manage one of your triggers more effectively?

_____

_____

_____

_____

_____

THE BOTTOM LINE

In any challenging situation, if you're not happy with the results you're getting, you have two choices:

1. Change the way you think and behave to get different results.

2. Settle for the results you're getting based on the way you think and behave.

Unfortunately, it doesn't work any other way. It doesn't matter if it's your marriage, your job, your kids, or any other life challenge. If you're not happy, you have to think and behave differently to get a different result, or stop complaining and being resentful for the results you're getting.

Change is scary, and it's usually made out of desperation, rather than inspiration. We get stuck in our job, our marriage, our routine. We stop dreaming about what our life can be, what we want it to be, and we settle for what we think we can get instead.

"Courage is the most important of all the virtues because without courage, you can't practice any other virtue consistently." —Maya Angelou

GETTING UNSTUCK

When we are young, we think we are invincible and can do anything (just ask my teenagers!). Somewhere along the way, that confidence and self-assurance starts getting knocked down, slowly eroding over time. We wake up one day and think, "I can't, I shouldn't, I couldn't possibly," and if we're not careful, it erodes our "courage bank account."

When our account is empty, we start to question ourselves and our choices. We second guess our gut instincts and overthink things. We become paralyzed with fear. We get stuck.

THE PIKE SYNDROME

In 1942, scientists at the Wolf Lake Hatchery in Michigan conducted an experiment with a Walleyed Pike. The carnivorous fish was placed in a large tank filled with minnows and as expected, it ate them. New minnows were then placed into the tank, only this time, they were inside a glass cylinder. The pike could see the minnows and in an effort to try to eat them, it kept ramming its head into the glass. It did this for hours and then finally settled on the bottom of the tank and gave up. Scientists then removed the glass cylinder so that the minnows could swim freely. Can you guess what happened next? The pike had already determined it wasn't able to eat the minnows. It continued to lie on the bottom of the tank and eventually starved to death. This has become known as the Pike Syndrome.

Our boundaries might not be a glass cylinder, but they are there, and we are all victims of the Pike Syndrome. Our fears, self-limiting beliefs, and perhaps even past experiences create imaginary barriers that we're convinced we can't break through. It's easy to give up and assume that there isn't another option. But there is.

OUR BRAINS ARE WIRED TO RESIST CHANGE

Our brains are lazy and will take the easy way out if we let them. They will take anything we repeatedly think, say, or do and turn it into a habit. It's easier for our brains to depend on habits because they don't have to work as hard. It's comfortable.

When we think and behave differently, new neuropathways are created, and the more we think that way, the stronger those neuropathways become.

"I can't do it anymore." That was what I was guilty of telling myself every day. "I can't do this. I'm tired. I'm done." I can't remember how many times I said it or thought it, but it was enough to create a pretty strong pathway. Every time I said it, I had a small pity party. My life wasn't fair. I couldn't accomplish my goals because of my situation at home. This was just my new reality. I said it so many times I started to believe it. And that is how the vicious cycle begins. We habituate our way into being stuck or losing sight of our courage.

We don't get stuck overnight. We slowly dig a rut that gets deeper every time we think or behave the same way, and a rut is just a grave with no ends.

It's easy to get complacent and content with the status quo. Courage means taking risks, going after what you really want, and pushing yourself out of your comfort zone. Most people hold back because they can't figure out how they are going to accomplish their goals. Thankfully, you don't have to know how because that's not the way your brain works. If you have a clear picture of your goal and believe that it's possible to achieve it, your brain will work backward to find ways to make it happen. I explain more about setting and accomplishing goals in my book *52 Strategies for Life, Love & Work*.

"Your life does not get better by chance, it gets better by change." —Jim Rohn

Flex Your Courage Muscles

Where are you stuck? What patterns have you settled into that may be holding you back? What imaginary barriers have you created for yourself?

_____

_____

_____

_____

_____

What can you do to break through these self-limiting barriers?

_____

_____

_____

_____

_____

WHERE COURAGE IS BORN

We are not born with courage or bravery. These attributes are not inherent or genetic characteristics pre-determined in our DNA. Courage is developed and built upon throughout a lifetime. Think of it as a byproduct of all that life presents to us—the victories and the losses. Dealing with heartache, pain, or grief can diminish our confidence in a heartbeat. When our physical or emotional well-being becomes fragile, we become vulnerable and less confident.

How we identify with courage will shift throughout our lifetime—guided by the ever-changing dynamics of circumstances, age, and experiences.

Flex Your Courage Muscles

At what point in your life did you feel most courageous? The least?

_____

_____

_____

_____

_____

_____

_____

_____

"We don't develop courage by being happy every day. We develop it by surviving difficult times and challenging adversity." —Barbara De Angelis

YOUR INNER CRITIC

I have the opportunity to meet and visit with incredible people all over the world. Some are upbeat, happy, and positive, while others are frustrated, fearful, and full of regret. I've tried to pay attention and look for patterns.

I've come to realize that yes, some people are genetically blessed. Their happiness set point is higher.[3] It's just like women who are tall, thin, and lean, yet can eat anything they want (those women really tick me off). Yet despite genetic factors, much of our experience comes from how we've been conditioned to think.

Self-limiting beliefs can stem from small or large conversations or experiences we've had throughout our lives. From a young age, we are taught to believe what our parents, caregivers, and teachers tell us.

We can all probably recall a childhood experience that had a big effect on us. Mine was my eighth grade algebra teacher, Mrs. Wilson, who definitely didn't help in my development or self-esteem. I had a really hard time with math. I was a perfectionist even back then, and I was afraid to fail. The combination of the two led me to ask a lot of questions. After a little time went by, it was obvious that Mrs. Wilson was not happy with my questions. She glared at me with a look I can still see to this day, then she asked the class to respond with, "Nooooooo Annnnneeee" every time I asked another question. I practically had to get therapy to get through the rest of math in high school and college.

While hopefully not that traumatizing, memories of hurtful comments, interactions, or even looks are something we all have. These can have a profound effect on our self-image.

And while the people around us certainly help shape our perceptions, much of our current reality is shaped by what we tell ourselves. The people who seem naturally "happier," also send themselves different messages.

This is easy to understand theoretically, but when we're in it, or when we're down, sad, and hopeless, it's really hard to do.

---

[3] Shawn Achor, *The Happiness Advantage: The Seven Principles of Positive Psychology That Fuel Success and Performance at Work* (New York: Crown Business, 2010).

The Two Words That Kill Courage

The two words that kill courage: *what if*? "What if I can't do it?" "What if I'm not smart enough?" "What if I don't have what it takes?" "What if…"

And if you're so inclined, I would also suggest dropping *should, can't,* and *impossible,* but the two words that you must avoid—the biggest courage destroyers—are *what if.*

So many times when we have an idea of something we want to do or try, we immediately go to "yeah, but what if…" We have created the habit of second guessing ourselves before we ever get started. Negative self-talk and doubt are the enemy of excellence.

I get caught in "what ifs" all the time. "What if Evan will have to struggle like this his entire life?" "What if I get sick again?" "What if…"

I've learned to challenge this voice, and so can you. These are the times when you need to muster all the courage you can to quiet your own negative chatter so you can bring yourself back and focus on what you can control—right now.

Flex Your Courage Muscles

Can you identify any people or situations that cause you to doubt yourself? Who or what are they?

_____

_____

_____

_____

_____

How Do You Talk to Yourself about Yourself?

Shifting your thinking doesn't happen overnight. It takes practice. Would you talk to your best friend the way you talk to yourself? If your friend came to you, sharing the challenges you are facing, what advice would you give?

Although simple in concept, shifting our thoughts can be extraordinarily difficult. We have conditioned ourselves to think the way we do. If we want to behave differently we have to think differently. We have to retrain our brains and form new habits. Thinking and behaving differently than we have in the past requires courage. It requires us to be thankful for what we have, to appreciate the little things, and to step outside of our comfort zone to look for the right things.

When we talk to ourselves, it's easy to go back to what we have habitually said. It takes practice to send ourselves new, more productive messages.

"We are what we repeatedly do. Excellence, then, is not an act, but a habit." —Aristotle

Sending the Right Messages

It might be unrealistic to jump from one extreme to the other; however, moving to a more realistic statement can be very powerful in your journey to find your courage.

For example, I used to think to myself, "This sucks. Why me? It's not fair!" As true as these statements might have been, they certainly weren't serving me.

It wasn't realistic for me to think, "I am the luckiest mom in the world! I love having a child with mental illness!" or "I'm super excited about facial paralysis!" but I was able to shift away from those thoughts. I began to use three little sayings regularly:

- I've got this.
- All I can do is all I can do.
- It is what it is. And it will become what I make it.

Here are some additional phrases and affirmations that help me:

- I have handled everything that has come my way so far. I will handle this, too.
- I believe in myself and my abilities.
- I choose to see the good in things.
- I am grateful for the blessings in my life.
- I eliminate obstacles and negativity around me.
- I embrace opportunities with an open heart and open mind.
- I feel better when I help others.
- I take risks and get out of my comfort zone.

Flex Your Courage Muscles

What negative thoughts could be getting in your way? How can you replace them with more positive or realistic thoughts?

Current Thought	More Positive, Realistic Thought
Examples:	
• "I could never do that."	• "I've never done that. I'm willing to give it a try."
• "I don't know how I will..."	
• "I'm too busy."	• "I will figure it out. I always do."
	• "I make time for what's important to me."

Now, write some of your current, negative thoughts and replace them with realistic or positive thoughts.

Current Thought	More Positive, Realistic Thought
• _____	• _____
• _____	• _____
• _____	• _____
• _____	• _____

Continued on the next page.

Flex Your Courage Muscles *Continued from the previous page.*

Write a few statements or affirmations that can help you when your courage is in question.

_____

_____

_____

_____

_____

_____

_____

_____

_____

_____

"To share your weakness is to make yourself vulnerable; to make yourself vulnerable is to show your strength." —Criss Jami

Zero In On the Good Stuff

We have the ability to filter out counterproductive stimuli, making it easier to zero in on the good stuff and keep our point of view on a positive course, but it takes practice.

For example, if you are looking for notes on your desk, you may remember that you wrote them in red ink, or that there is an orange sticky note on the page. While you flip through your piles of paper, your brain is searching for the red ink or orange sticky note. It lets everything else slip through because it's only looking for something specific. If I asked you to find the notes written in green, you would have to flip through the papers again because you weren't looking for that the first time.

When we are caught in a negative thought cycle, it's easy to look for (and find) all of the things that are not fair. It's easy to slip further into sadness, loneliness, and grief. The opposite is also true.

When we find even the smallest things for which to be grateful (the parking spot up front, making a green light, a sale on the apples we like, etc.), it's amazing how our minds open and start to zero in on these things.

For a long time, I lived in fear. Sometimes physical fear, but often fear of what might happen down the road with Evan, my career, my family, my health, and on and on. When I decided to live courageously, my mind shifted almost immediately. Instead of my thought, "What will I do if Evan can never live on his own?" I started to think, "I've made it this far. I can handle anything." Something as simple as shifting your thoughts can transform fear into courage.

Being Vulnerable

I'm a big Brené Brown fan. She has done some great research around shame, vulnerability, and courage. She explains that we can choose courage or we can choose comfort, but we can't have both. Brown asserts that vulnerability is the greatest measure of courage.

When I speak, I share the nitty-gritty aspects of my life. People often ask how I can be so open, so vulnerable. I'll be honest, part of it is cathartic. It needs to come out somehow, and I've found this to be a productive outlet. But mostly, it's because people tell me how much it means to them, and how much it helps them.

Vulnerability can be scary. We crave certainty, and courage requires us to get comfortable with ambiguity and the unknown. It means that you are willing to risk being hurt, willing to forge ahead into the unknown because ahead is the only way to go. It means you don't have all of the answers, but you keep looking. Vulnerability is the true measure of courage.

"If you have the courage to begin, you have the courage to succeed." —David Viscott

DISCOMFORT IS A CATALYST FOR GROWTH

Making changes is often awkward, difficult, and uncomfortable. It's also where courage happens. I stumbled across a video by Rabbi Dr. Abraham Twerski who explained how lobsters grow.[4] Besides being absolutely delicious, these sea creatures have got this whole courage thing figured out. When a lobster grows, its shell becomes constricting and uncomfortable. The shell doesn't grow with the lobster, so in order to grow the lobster has to shed its shell to grow a bigger one. When it's time to upgrade, it just scurries under a few rocks and hangs out vulnerably while it waits for its new shell to grow. It continues to do this its whole life, sometimes more than 20 times. The only way for the lobster to grow is for it to be uncomfortable and vulnerable while it's making a bigger, better shell.

Courage is not the absence of fear. Courage is being afraid and working through the discomfort. Just like the lobster, it means taking off your shell and being vulnerable. Courage means you allow challenge and adversity to be a catalyst to help you grow strong enough.

We don't like leaving our comfort zones or forming new habits, even if the new habits are for our own good. However, getting back in the game and building lasting confidence will require change, and most likely some discomfort.

Being courageous isn't hard when you're happy and everything is hunky dory. It is when you're exhausted, emotional, angry, and life is far away from what you had planned that finding your courage gets hard. Courage is how we choose to act during these times.

Being fearless and having courage are not mutually exclusive. In fact, true courage means being afraid and forging ahead anyway.

When I had facial paralysis, I cringed every time I looked in the mirror. Everywhere I went, I was so focused on how people looked at me, that's all I saw. A meeting planner at a conference called and asked me to speak about overcoming adversity. Ironically, she had no idea that any of this had happened to me. She was talking about the adversity I face raising Evan. When I explained everything that had happened recently with the tumor and facial paralysis, she said, "That's an even better message!"

---

[4]   Rabbi Dr. Abraham Twerski on Responding to Stress, available at https://www.youtube.com/watch?v=3aDXM5H-Fuw.

My initial instinct was to say no. I was about to start radiation and I was still recovering from surgery. I certainly wasn't up for travel, and I didn't even want pictures taken of me with my face looking like it did, let alone show it to an audience of a few thousand people.

As I started to write the email declining the engagement, I was overtaken by sadness. I just sat there and cried. I cried in part because of everything that had happened, but part of me was crying out of pure fear. After I let myself have a good cry, I decided that I can't tell other people to find their courage if I'm not willing to find mine.

I picked up the phone and called the event planner. I explained that physically, I really wasn't able to travel yet but asked if she would be willing to let me make a video. She was thrilled at the idea, and told me she thought I was brave.

It occurred to me in that moment that having courage didn't mean I wasn't afraid. I was petrified. Courage meant I did it anyway.

"Don't be afraid of your fears. They're not there to scare you. They're there to let you know that something is worth it." —C. JoyBell C.

Overcoming Fear

Fear is a normal part of a full life, but when it begins to impede your ability to live that life to its fullest, it's time to do something about it.

No one strategy works for everyone. Here are a few steps I have found helpful:

- Identify your fear and describe it. Name it.
- Pay attention to your physical reactions. Simply recognizing increased heart rate or sweaty palms can alert you to take a few deep breaths.
- Identify the root cause of your fear.
- Reframe your thoughts and talk to yourself. I say, "Ok, Anne. You've got this."
- Take action. Even if it's something small.

Before you can face down your fears, you must focus on what is truly important, and on the things you can directly affect. This takes thinking logically, no matter how creative you are. This doesn't happen overnight—it's a process.

A few things to know about the process:

- **Having the answers is not required!** Initiating smart questions will stimulate courageous behavior. Make a list of really good questions and let those be your guide (e.g., What thoughts are keeping me stuck? What's the worst case scenario? What's the best case scenario?). Stop worrying about what the outcome is going to look like, because sometimes there is just no telling how things will shape up. Don't force it.

- **Stop looking to the past.** Who you were in the past does not have to dictate who you are capable of becoming tomorrow. This is a big part of finding your courage. Courageous people blaze new trails and territory. What will yours be?

- **Time really does heal.** Give yourself the gift of time to find your courage and build resilience to overcome obstacles and challenges in your life.

- **Stop comparing yourself to others!** You have no idea what other people's lives are about, where they've been, or what they are facing. Everybody has hardships; they're just not advertising them. Redirect your thinking to become the best version of *you*.

- **Look within yourself.** What are you really afraid of? How much is anxiety and emotionally driven fear? What are action steps that you can work through instead of being afraid? It's helpful to distinguish the emotional from the logical.

REFUSE TO LET FEAR HOLD YOU BACK

Emotional wounds will surely remind us of where we've been, but our personal history doesn't have to dictate where we're headed. How do we keep getting up after we have been knocked down? It is because we are resilient, and we do what needs to be done.

Anyone can give up; it's the easiest thing in the world to do. But to hold it together when everyone else would understand if you fell apart, that is true strength. That is grit. That is courage and resilience. And that equals triumph.

Flex Your Courage Muscles

Identify a current fear and describe it.

_____

_____

_____

_____

What is happening physically when you experience the fear?

_____

_____

_____

_____

Identify the root cause of your fear. What is this really about?

_____

_____

_____

_____

Continued on the next page.

Flex Your Courage Muscles *Continued from previous page.*

How can you reframe your thinking? What can you say to yourself (pretend you're comforting a friend who's experiencing the same thing)?

_____

_____

_____

_____

What action can you take right now?

_____

_____

_____

_____

"Courage doesn't always roar. Sometimes courage is the quiet voice at the end of the day that says I'll try again tomorrow." —Mary Anne Rachmacher

Courage Is Conquering Fear through Inspiration

When you are in crisis or in the midst of desperation, you are challenged to tap into strength that you may not realize you have. Finding courage in these times is no fun, but it frequently happens this way.

Finding courage and strength because you are inspired is the key. When you are passionate enough or motivated enough to do or have something, you find a way to make it happen. Sometimes, you just have to get out of your own way.

What will you do to begin your journey? Here are just a few ideas:

- Embark on a spiritual journey.
- Join a support group.
- Take classes to further your education.

- Renew a relationship.
- Join a health club.
- Take a vacation.
- Initiate a financial plan.
- Plan a family reunion.
- Get a health check-up.
- Try something adventurous.
- Volunteer.
- Revive a hobby you used to enjoy or start a new one.
- Support a cause you believe in.

"Go confidently in the direction of your dreams. Live the life you've imagined." —Henry David Thoreau

Flex Your Courage Muscles

How will you allow inspiration to guide you?

_____

_____

_____

_____

IT'S YOUR TURN

Perhaps you are now seeking a kind of courage you've never sought before, or maybe you are not sure why you lost the bravery you once possessed. It doesn't always require stressful circumstances or something traumatic to steal your courage. Just by being insulated in a comfortable, safe environment for a period of time can diminish the need for courage. Status quo can equal complacency; complacency can kill courage.

People often ask me, "Anne, how do you stay so motivated?" My question is, "What makes you think I stay motivated?" Trust me, my life isn't all butterflies and daisies. I don't "stay" motivated—I choose motivation. Courage means making the choice, even when you don't feel like it. It also means giving yourself permission to know when it's time to choose motivation, and when it's time to give yourself a break. This is a journey. You will take two steps forward and one step back. Whatever you do, don't give up.

Where could you use some courage right now? Imagine what your life could look like if you removed all of the barriers. What would you do? How would you feel? What would it look like? What could you accomplish if you lived up to your true potential?

Flex Your Courage Muscles

Describe a time when your strength was tested. What did you do to get through it?

_____

_____

_____

_____

_____

Continued on the next page.

Flex Your Courage Muscles *Continued from previous page.*

Identify something that can motivate and inspire you when your courage is in question.

_____

_____

_____

_____

_____

What can you do each day to remind yourself to *choose* to stay motivated and inspired?

_____

_____

_____

_____

_____

"You have to accept whatever comes and the only important thing is that you meet it with courage and with the best that you have to give." —Eleanor Roosevelt

JOURNAL YOUR THOUGHTS

Think of all of this as embarking on a new beginning. Because we know that change takes place in repetitive small fragments over a period of time, monitoring and noting your progress needs to become a daily habit to slowly etch these changes into your brain. Don't forget that you, and you alone, are in command of your habits. Also remember to keep your expectations realistic. Before you know it, your point of view will gradually evolve, and it will become easier to maintain the new habits.

At the end of each day, identify something that happened that you can attribute to strengthening your confidence or something that made you feel courageous. Maybe it's a conversation you had or a random act of kindness you performed for someone you didn't even know. Whatever it is, write it down. I believe that we find what we look for. There is no better way to find your courage and strength than by looking for it.

Flex Your Courage Muscles

What did you do today that took strength and courage? It could be as simple as challenging a negative thought, standing up for yourself, or having a difficult conversation.

_____

_____

_____

What strategies will you apply from these lessons to help grow your courage?

_____

_____

_____

How will you track your progress and celebrate success?

_____

_____

_____

PART 2:
RESILIENCE

I was recently speaking at a conference in Philadelphia, and while doing a book signing after the presentation, a man walked up, put his hands on the table, looked right at me and said, "Dude. I thought my life was crappy. How do you keep getting back up after you've been knocked down?" I wasn't sure whether to take it as an insult or a compliment, but the question stuck with me—how do any of us get back up when we've been knocked down? It is because we are resilient by nature.

Resilience is defined as *the ability to recover from or adjust easily to misfortune or change.*[5] Basically, it's the ability to get back up after you've been knocked down. I used to think resilience was in your genetics, like skinny thighs. You either have it or you don't. But what I've come to realize, to appreciate, is that resilience is a set of skills, rather than a disposition or personality type. We can grow and cultivate resilience so that we cannot only make it through hard times, but become stronger as a result.

Not a day goes by when we aren't affected by misfortune, tragedy, or just a plain old challenge. Maybe you lost your job, got a divorce, or declared bankruptcy. Or maybe you or a loved one has been diagnosed with a serious illness, or you have a child with a learning disability. Any one of these or countless other situations can position us for traumatic, life-changing events. Some situations seem small and insignificant, while others can become overwhelmingly difficult, if not seemingly impossible, to process and move past. It's easy to become overwhelmed.

---

[5] Merriam-Webster's Collegiate Dictionary, 11th ed., s.v. "resilience."

A MAGIC PILL

I read this great article about our capacity to remember the good and bad things in our lives and how it shapes how resilient we can become.

Imagine you're the manager of a café. It stays open late and the neighborhood has gone quiet by the time you lock the doors. You put the evening's earnings into a bank bag, tuck that into your backpack, and head home. It's a short walk through a poorly lit park. And there, next to the pond, you hear footsteps behind you. Before you can turn around, a man sprints up and stabs you in the stomach. When you fall to the ground, he kicks you, grabs your backpack, and runs off. Fortunately, a bystander calls an ambulance which takes you, bleeding and shaken, to the nearest hospital.

The emergency room physician stitches you up and tells you that, aside from the pain and a bit of blood loss, you're in good shape. Then she sits down and looks you in the eye. She tells you that people who live through a traumatic event like yours often develop post-traumatic stress disorder (PTSD). The condition can be debilitating, resulting in flashbacks that prompt you to relive the trauma over and over. It can cause irritation, anxiety, angry outbursts and a magnified fear response. But she has a pill you can take right now that will decrease your recall of the night's events—and thus the fear and other emotions associated with it—and guard against the potential effects of PTSD without completely erasing the memory itself.

Would you take that pill?

When Elizabeth Loftus, a psychologist at the University of California, Irvine, asked nearly 1,000 people a similar question, more than 80 percent said: 'No.' They would rather retain all memory and emotion of that day, even if it came with a price.[6]

---

[6] Lauren Gravitz, "The Possibility of Erasing Negative Memories," *It's Interesting*, August 5, 2016, available at https://its-interesting.com/category/uncategorized/page/2/.

We achieve strength through struggle. When we make it through a trauma, crisis, or stressful time, we learn something. It is called post-traumatic growth. It's like flexing your resilience muscles. Although you don't usually see the lesson at the time, you are able to look back with perspective and learn from it.

Sonja Lyubomirsky, a professor of psychology at the University of California Riverside, says that when upheaval strikes, we should consider how we have improved as a result.[7] Her research has shown that women diagnosed with breast cancer found numerous positive emotions as a result, including re-evaluating true priorities and improved self-confidence.

The bottom line is that resilient people don't let adversity define them. They perceive pain and misfortune as temporary. They don't waste difficult experiences and difficult times. They use them as a catalyst for growth.

CHARACTERISTICS OF RESILIENCE

When we don't have the proper tools, we don't have adequate means to face the obstacles life will inevitably present. Most of us are not intentionally taught resilience; rather, we gain it through life experience. Given that the average person experiences five to six traumas in his/her life, these seem like pretty necessary skills. I wish I had learned them in school. I use resilience way more than I use algebra. Fortunately, resilience is a skill that can be cultivated, practiced, and honed.

The first step is to identify how resilient you currently are. Dr. Richard Davidson, a neuroscientist at the University of Wisconsin Madison, explained that a good way to gauge your current level of resilience is to consider how you react when things don't go your way.[8] This research shows that the way we cope with little stressors strongly predicts how we will deal with big ones.

---

[7] *The Science of Happiness: New Discoveries for a More Joyful Life* (New York: Time, 2016).

[8] Richard Davidson and Sharon Begley, *The Emotional Life of Your Brain: How Its Unique Patterns Affect the Way You Think, Feel, and Live—and How You Can Change Them* (New York: Plume, 2012).

RESILIENCE SELF-ASSESSMENT

Take a moment complete this self-assessment to help determine your current level of resilience.

Circle the following for each statement:

4 = Always   3 = Sometimes   2 = Rarely   1 = Never

1.	I adapt to changing situations easily.	4	3	2	1
2.	I notice when things are going poorly in my relationships.	4	3	2	1
3.	I take full responsibility for what goes right and wrong in my life.	4	3	2	1
4.	I set and achieve goals.	4	3	2	1
5.	I challenge myself and try new things.	4	3	2	1
6.	I believe difficult situations make me stronger.	4	3	2	1
7.	I am self-confident and believe in my abilities.	4	3	2	1
8.	I am satisfied and proud of the life I live.	4	3	2	1
9.	I assess most situations from different points of view.	4	3	2	1
10.	I "read" people well and trust my intuition.	4	3	2	1
11.	I respond well in a crisis.	4	3	2	1
12.	I embrace spontaneity.	4	3	2	1
13.	I know my strengths and focus on them.	4	3	2	1
14.	I find ways to experience humor and laughter.	4	3	2	1
15.	I learn something from my setbacks.	4	3	2	1
16.	I am self-confident.	4	3	2	1
17.	I surround myself with positive people.	4	3	2	1
18.	I take time to express gratitude and appreciation.	4	3	2	1
19.	I take time to grieve.	4	3	2	1
20.	I eat well, get enough rest, and exercise.	4	3	2	1

Scoring:

70-80 points = Appreciate your resilience. Keep doing what you're doing and look for subtle ways to boost resilience, and take time to teach others how to bounce back.

60-69 points = You already get back up. There are a few things you can do to improve your current level of resilience and get up faster. Keep reading.

50-59 points = Pay attention to your recovery time. What can you do to shorten the time you're down?

Fewer than 50 points = This is your opportunity to practice resilience. Pick any item where you scored 3 or lower and identify an action step you can take.

Although we all experience setbacks, sadness, stress, and loss, the people who tend to navigate these challenges more easily share similar characteristics. Highly resilient people...

- Have a clear vision and goals.
- Stay connected and build strong, positive relationships.
- Practice mindfulness.
- Find humor in the little things and do not take themselves too seriously.
- Embrace change as an opportunity.
- Respond intentionally rather than react emotionally.
- Give of themselves to help others.
- Consider adversity as a challenge and opportunity.
- Process grief.
- Focus on their strengths.
- Think optimistically.
- View themselves as fighters, not victims.
- Have high emotional intelligence (EI) and cultivate self-awareness.
- Learn from their experiences to guide future behavior.
- Take care of their mental, emotional, physical, and spiritual health.
- Perceive bad times as temporary.
- Focus on what they can control.
- Avoid complaining, criticizing, and complacency.
- Stretch out of their comfort zone and take risks.
- Surround themselves with positive people.
- Have strong values that guide behavior.

Flex Your Resilience Muscles

Based on your resilience self-assessment, what action step will you take to build resilience?

_____

_____

_____

_____

From the list on the previous page, which characteristics come easily for you?

_____

_____

_____

_____

Which characteristics do you feel you are lacking? How can you make improvements?

_____

_____

_____

_____

ARE YOU GREEN AND GROWING OR RIPE AND ROTTING?

There's an old saying: we are either green and growing or ripe and rotting. We're either getting better, or we are headed in the other direction. Staying stagnant is not an option. We typically respond to challenges in one of two ways:

- We accept our challenges and remain open to learning lessons.
- We resist our opportunities to grow.

Building resilience requires that we forge ahead, constantly looking for new ways to improve and better ourselves.

Flex Your Resilience Muscles

In what areas of your life have you gotten stagnant or complacent?

_____

_____

_____

_____

What will you do about it?

_____

_____

_____

_____

FAILURE LEADS TO SUCCESS

Fail, learn, and try again. I don't know any highly successful people who haven't suffered setbacks throughout their life and career. All of them can name numerous failures. Dr. Seuss was rejected 27 times before publishing his first book in 1937. He then went on to sell 600 million books worldwide.

It's a fact. Successful people fail more than unsuccessful people. Successful people take risks, they view failure as a learning tool, and they practice resilience.

In an effort to protect ourselves, we often play it safe or don't stretch for what we really want. When we do take that leap and don't succeed, it's easy to throw up our hands and give up.

Truly resilient people stick with it. They continue to take risks and view failure as an opportunity to learn what not to repeat.

"The greatest glory in living lies not in never falling, but in rising every time we fall." —Nelson Mandela

It's a Learning Opportunity

It's natural when faced with an overwhelming situation to feel defeated, but people who practice resilience learn to see the situation a bit differently. They have their initial feelings, process them, and then look at the problem and say, "What is this teaching me? What can I learn from this?" They choose to use failure and adversity as learning opportunities.

Evan goes to a school for children with emotional disturbances. The faculty and staff are incredibly well trained and do an amazing job with behavioral interventions. One of the things they stress to the kids is that making mistakes isn't always bad. Many times, these are life's greatest learning opportunities.

Recently Evan got angry and stormed out of the house. Normally, when he gets angry, he walks down to the creek or the neighborhood pond. When he didn't come back after 10 minutes, we started looking for him. And looking. And looking. As panic set in, we had a whole team of people searching for him, and I had all kinds of horrible worst-case scenarios running through my mind. More than two hours later, Evan called me from the leasing office of a random apartment complex that he'd walked to (more than three miles away!).

Now, I'm not proud of what happened next, but in the spirit of transparency, I'll share it anyway. I drove like a bat out of hell to the apartment complex, got out of the car at the leasing office, saw Evan, and lost my freaking mind. I was still in my pajamas, it was 30 degrees outside, I had been crying for two hours, and I screamed, "Where the hell have you been? Do you have ANY idea how scared we have been? You are in SO much trouble!" The poor leasing manager probably thought I was a nut job. Without missing a beat, Evan looked at me with his big blue eyes, then at the leasing manager, and then back at me and in his cutest voice said, "Mom, I'm not sure I should get in trouble. This has been a valuable learning opportunity." Smart ass.

I wish I could say I just jumped back up and used it as a learning opportunity immediately, but it took a little time to process. I was angry, I was hurt, and I was sad. I allowed myself time to feel those things, and then I got back up. That is courage. That is resilience. That is what triumph looks like for me. It doesn't mean I don't have crappy days. Trust me, I have crappy days. It means I figure out what went wrong and try not to repeat it.

In fact, finding meaning from challenging situations can buffer against negative feelings and their consequences. For the longest time, I was stuck in "why me?" mode. When I share our story, people thank me for letting them know they are not alone. Knowing I'm making a difference has become my meaning. Evan also feels a huge sense of pride knowing his story is helping others. This is post-traumatic growth, and it is a defining characteristic of resilience.

Everyday Setbacks

Significant events can certainly shake us to our core, but it's often the more mundane, everyday experiences that slowly erode our confidence and self-esteem. We are inundated with more information than we can process, overwhelmed with stimulus from technology, and bombarded with to-do lists, tasks, and responsibilities. We are literally accessible all the time. Simply surviving our everyday lives requires mental toughness, strength, and grit.

Life challenges are not just situational. In fact, some of the toughest challenges are all about our mental attitude. It requires a conscious choice to focus on the right attitudes. It means choosing not to be dishonest, jealous, selfish, angry, negative, greedy, judgmental, self-centered, insecure, manipulative, moody, etc. It means forgiving yourself when you feel this way.

Flex Your Resilience Muscles

What attitudes are currently contributing to your resilience, and what attitudes could be holding you back?

_____

_____

_____

_____

Write five words that you would use to describe yourself, your courage, and your strength.

1. _____

2. _____

3. _____

4. _____

5. _____

Then, without sharing your words, ask someone you love or care about to write five words they would use to describe you, your courage, and your strength.

Next, compare your lists. We don't always see ourselves the way we are seen by others. In general, we think and behave like the kind of person we think we are. Courageous and resilient people think and behave like the kind of person they want to become.

What attitudes or behaviors do you have that need a resilience makeover?

_____

_____

_____

_____

EMOTIONAL INTELLIGENCE AND RESILIENCE

Your ability to become and remain resilient is directly related to your emotional intelligence. Emotional intelligence is the ability to understand your mood and emotions, be aware of the moods and emotions of others, and to use this awareness to guide your behavior. Emotional intelligence determines how you interact with others, manage relationships, stay motivated, make decisions, manage your emotions, influence others, and much more. The stronger your emotions, the more likely they are to dictate your behavior.

Your Brain on Stress

When you are under stress, the emotional center of your brain (specifically the amygdala) lights up, shooting cortisol and adrenaline through your brain. This was originally intended to help us freeze, run away, or fight an impending attacker; the same process happens when we face an emotional setback or threat.

Understanding your reactions to stress in difficult situations is critical. There are physiological responses, such as breathing difficulties, hair loss, bleeding gums, aches, pains, high blood pressure, etc., and then there are the psychological responses, including anxiety, depression, nervous ticks, etc. When you identify how you respond to stress, you can begin to find ways to proactively manage it.

Flex Your Resilience Muscles

How does stress affect you physically (e.g., tightness in your chest, sweating, knots in your stomach, headaches, etc.)?

_____

_____

_____

_____

Continued on the next page.

Flex Your Resilience Muscles *Continued from previous page.*

How does stress affect you psychologically and emotionally (e.g., sadness, anxiety, feeling out of control)?

_____

_____

_____

_____

How have you learned to de-stress (e.g., laughing, meditating, practicing yoga, reading, etc.)?

_____

_____

_____

_____

EMOTIONAL INTELLIGENCE SELF-ASSESSMENT

There are many things that build emotional intelligence (EI), and it can be measured in various ways. Take a moment to complete this self-assessment to identify areas of strength and opportunity in your own emotional intelligence.

Circle the following for each statement:

4 = Always   3 = Sometimes   2 = Rarely   1 = Never

1.	I am innately aware of my feelings when I feel them.	4	3	2	1
2.	I am considerate and can clearly express what I am feeling when I am with others.	4	3	2	1
3.	I can easily tell people what I am feeling or thinking during difficult discussions.	4	3	2	1
4.	I think before I speak and I am sensitive to others' feelings.	4	3	2	1
5.	I balance my need to speak up with others' need to speak.	4	3	2	1
6.	I build relationships that are mutually gratifying and satisfying.	4	3	2	1
7.	I easily and intuitively relate to how others may be feeling.	4	3	2	1
8.	When someone disagrees with me, I listen to their point of view.	4	3	2	1
9.	When I am upset, I find ways to communicate my needs.	4	3	2	1
10.	I assess my options, choosing the best alternative under pressure.	4	3	2	1
11.	I control any impulses to act too hastily when I'm under pressure.	4	3	2	1
12.	I cope with stress in a positive way, examining possibilities.	4	3	2	1
13.	I am flexible in the face of changes at home and at work.	4	3	2	1
14.	I take time for myself regularly and do the things I enjoy.	4	3	2	1
15.	I am optimistic, even in the face of tough challenges.	4	3	2	1

Interpreting Your Self-Assessment

In general, higher scores (3 or 4) indicate stronger emotional intelligence. Although all 4s may indicate "wishful thinking," too many 1s and 2s could mean you are being too hard on yourself. To confirm your assessment results, ask a trusted friend, family member, or colleague how they would rank you in these areas.

Building your emotional intelligence is a learned behavior and skill that takes practice and time. Below are a few suggestions for improvement. Research shows it takes three to six months of practicing an emotional-based behavior in order to begin changing it. Tell people you trust about your goals and objectives to increase support and commitment from those around you.

I've broken down the interpretation of the self-assessment into three parts:

- Emotional Expression
- Stress and Conflict
- Mood and Attitude

Emotional Expression

This is the foundation of EI. If these scores are low, start working on building emotional awareness by assessing your feelings throughout the day, before making decisions, and before and after conversations.

1. I am innately aware of my feelings when I feel them.
2. I am considerate and can clearly express what I am feeling when I am with others.
3. I can easily tell people what I am feeling or thinking during difficult discussions.
4. I think before I speak and I am sensitive to others' feelings.

The following statements provide insight into your level of assertiveness and relationship building ability. Being able to assert yourself is critical to getting your needs met, as well as influencing others.

5. I balance my need to speak up with others' need to speak.
6. I build relationships that are mutually gratifying and satisfying.
7. I easily and intuitively relate to how others may be feeling.

Relationship building is critical to success at work and in life. If you scored a 1 or 2, be more curious, ask more questions, and find out where the other person is coming from.

Stress and Conflict

Communicating under stress or during conflict is a critical skill set. It requires good communication, an awareness of emotions, and conflict resolution skills. If you scored low on a question, always start a disagreement with "What do you think?" and don't share your point of view until you understand theirs.

8. When someone disagrees with me, I listen to their point of view.

9. When I am upset, I find ways to communicate my needs.

10. I assess my options, choosing the best alternative under pressure.

11. I control any impulses to act too hastily when I'm under pressure.

12. I cope with stress in a positive way, examining possibilities.

Everyone needs help dealing with stress now and then. Questions 10 and 11, in particular, come down to training yourself to be calm and managing your emotions.

Mood and Attitude

Your general mood and attitude influences your overall EI effectiveness. When you are rested and relaxed, you are much more likely to handle upsetting situations calmly. These statements provide insight into your moods and attitudes.

13. I am flexible in the face of changes at home and at work.

14. I take time for myself regularly and do the things I enjoy.

15. I am optimistic, even in the face of tough challenges.

Flex Your Resilience Muscles

What are your greatest emotional intelligence strengths?

_____

_____

_____

_____

What one or two areas would you like to improve?

_____

_____

_____

_____

What action(s) can you take to habituate a new thought or behavior?

_____

_____

_____

_____

BUILDING RESILIENCE

So much research is being done in the area of resilience, and there are many strategies that have proven successful. What works for some may not work for others. Dr. Dennis Charney, a psychiatrist and Dean of the Icahn School of Medicine, has studied resilience for more than two decades. He has found that there is not a one-size-fits-all approach; rather, each person must find what works best for them.[9] The following are strategies that have helped build my resilience.

---

[9] Steven M. Southwick and Dennis S. Charney, _Resilience: The Science of Mastering Life's Greatest Challenges_ (Cambridge, UK: Cambridge University Press, 2012).

Have a Vision and Goals

Having a clear vision of success and a well thought out strategy to achieve it is a great way to build resilience. Think of it like swimming in the ocean. It's easy to think you are swimming in a straight line, only to realize you've been carried away by the current. To ensure they are headed in the right direction, open water swimmers will often choose a buoy, lighthouse, or some other structure to aim for. That way, regardless of the tide and current, they know they are on the right track.

In the United States Army, Special Forces (SF) are an elite group of soldiers. SF are used for unconventional warfare, foreign defense, and counter-terrorism, among other things. The army provides these teams with high-level training, including the ability to build resilience. Special forces instructors teach soldiers to focus on goals and on the mission of the group as tools to manage fear and remain resilient, and studies have shown this strategy to be quite effective.[10]

From the time we are small children, we are taught that if we want to be successful, we have to keep our heads down and work hard. The only problem with that is that you could look up years later and realize you are nowhere near your desired destination. Having a vision of success is your lighthouse. It allows you to work hard while maintaining focus on the right things.

We love to do puzzles at our house. It's a simple activity where everyone can be involved, and we don't have to do it all at once. If we have 10 or 15 minutes, we'll grab a seat at the dining room table and work on a puzzle. Sometimes I catch myself stumped on where a piece fits and then realize that the picture is right on the box. I just have to follow the picture.

Having a vision for your life is the same thing. Without a clear picture of where you want to go, it's impossible to create a path to get there.

If you don't have a clear vision of success, that is okay, too. Think about how you would like to feel. What would you like coming home at the end of the day to look like? How do you want your mornings to go?

---

[10] Ibid.

Envisioning these things doesn't make you more resilient. Being able to bounce back because you believe this future is possible—that is what makes you resilient.

Success isn't a straight line. You will stumble and get off track at times, but that doesn't mean you have to completely derail. The difference between those who are resilient and those who are not is whether or not they get back on track.

In my book *52 Strategies for Life, Love & Work*, I talk about creating a dream board. It's a visual guideline of what success looks like to you—and it can change over time. For example, for a long time, on my dream board I had pictures of India. What would be on yours?

Flex Your Resilience Muscles

How do you envision your future? What does success look like?

_____

_____

_____

_____

What can you start doing to make it a reality?

_____

_____

_____

_____

Focus on Your Strengths

Most of us have been taught that if we want to grow personally or professionally, we should figure out our weaknesses and improve upon them. That's great if we want to become miserable and mediocre. Resilient people identify their strengths and magnify them. This doesn't mean ignoring skills that need improvement or not learning new things.

It does mean that we stop beating ourselves up for who we're not and start appreciating ourselves for who we are. Focusing on our strengths can help us become more confident and resilient.

When our confidence is shaken, it is easy to struggle with identifying our strengths, and we lose sight of our greatest attributes. Proactively building resilience requires us to stop long enough to think about the big picture.

Willibald Ruch, a professor of psychology at the University of Zurich, studies character strength and happiness. He explains that people who consistently focus on their strengths experience less depression and more happiness.[11]

Flex Your Resilience Muscles

Take a moment to complete the following statements:

I feel most energized when...

_____

_____

_____

_____

_____

I feel most drained when...

_____

_____

_____

_____

_____

Continued on the next page.

---

[11] Fabian Gander, René T. Proyer, Willibald Ruch, and Tobias Wyss, "Strength-Based Positive Interventions: Further Evidence for Their Potential in Enhancing Well-Being and Alleviating Depression," *Journal of Happiness Studies* 14, no. 4 (2013): 1241-1259.

Flex Your Resilience Muscles *Continued from the previous page.*

People see the best of me when...

_____

_____

_____

_____

_____

People see the worst of me when...

_____

_____

_____

_____

_____

I can use my strengths by...

_____

_____

_____

_____

_____

I find fulfillment from...

_____

_____

_____

_____

_____

Continued on the next page.

The things that energize you are your strengths. Write down how you can do more of these things.

_____

_____

_____

_____

_____

The things that drain you are usually weaknesses. How can you spend less time doing these tasks, or even better, is there a way to use your strengths to get around them?

_____

_____

_____

_____

_____

Ask those closest to you to write what they believe are your greatest strengths. You will probably be surprised by all of the things they see in you.

If you have lost sight of your strengths, it's time to tackle this head on and take a hard look at everything that has made you who you are, warts and all.

Even if you are incredibly resilient, there will be times when getting back up will be harder than others. If you're willing to do the work, you can become more resilient.

The Company We Keep

A defining characteristic of resilient people is the type of people with whom they surround themselves. Some people (we all know a few) are what I call "drama starters." It's like there is always some breaking news story going on in their life. They thrive on getting people spun up. And if we're not careful, they can suck the energy right out of us.

It's time to take back control. People will not share their drama if you won't listen to it. You don't have to be rude—acknowledge what they said and change the subject, or simply excuse yourself because you are busy. Not your circus. Not your monkeys.

Then there are the haters, complainers, whiners, and everything in between. The more our inner circle is filled with positive, encouraging, and supportive people, the more resilient we will become.

Flex Your Resilience Muscles

Who should be in your inner circle? What can you do to spend more time with these people?

_____

_____

_____

_____

_____

Who should not be in your inner circle? What can you do to create distance?

_____

_____

_____

_____

Process Grief

In college, I took a class called Death, Dying, and Bereavement. We were introduced to the grief model by Elisabeth Kübler-Ross. I was later re-introduced to this model when I took classes from the National Alliance on Mental Illness (NAMI). (I credit my support group and my teachers at NAMI for helping me survive some of my roughest times.)

When we face a loss (any kind of loss), it's easy to want to run from the discomfort. It takes strength to process what is happening. Allowing ourselves the time and space to grieve is not a luxury, it is a requirement for resilience. Figure 1 below illustrates the process of grieving and the required steps.

Figure 1. The Grief Process

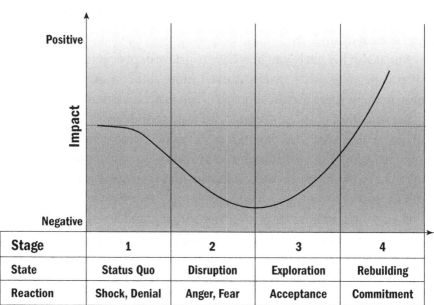

Stage	1	2	3	4
State	Status Quo	Disruption	Exploration	Rebuilding
Reaction	Shock, Denial	Anger, Fear	Acceptance	Commitment

Source: Adapted from Elisabeth Kübler-Ross, *On Death and Dying: What the Dying Have to Teach Doctors, Nurses, Clergy and Their Own Families* (New York: MacMillian Co., 1969).

You Can't Microwave Grief

All people grieve differently. Kübler-Ross developed a grief model with five stages: denial, anger, bargaining, depression, and finally, acceptance.[12] Unfortunately, grief is not a linear process. For me, raising a child with special needs means going through the grief cycle daily. I grieve for the child I thought I was going to have. I grieve the loss of the life I had imagined. I grieve for the struggles Evan will have to endure. At first, I experienced denial: *This can't be happening.* Then I got mad: *Why is this happening to me?* Next, I promised God that I would never do anything wrong or ask for anything ever again, if only this can change. Then I began to learn to manage around the situation, pulling on strength I never knew I had. The final stage, acceptance, is one that I find fleeting. The problem with grief is that you don't go through these stages one at a time, and just because you've been through one doesn't mean you won't experience it again.

And it's highly likely you may have to grieve or process multiple things at the same time. That makes it even more difficult and complicated. Unfortunately, there are no shortcuts. You just can't microwave grief.

Because grief is uncomfortable, we want to hide from it, thinking we will deal with it later. Only there is never a good time. Uncomfortable as it may be, until you go through the process, you won't truly recover. If you're angry, be angry. If you're sad, cry. And if you just want to scream, that's okay, too.

It was three or four days after my surgery, and I was sitting on the couch talking with my mom and Jay about my facial paralysis. I got really angry, threw a box of tissues across the room and yelled, "It isn't f*&%@ng fair!" Rather than tell me it was going to be okay, or list the reasons why I shouldn't feel the way I felt, they both looked at me and said, "You're right. It isn't f*&%@ng fair."

I just needed to get that out. Then, we all had a good laugh.

---

12 Elisabeth Kübler-Ross, *On Death and Dying: What the Dying Have to Teach Doctors, Nurses, Clergy and Their Own Families* (New York: MacMillian Co., 1969).

Flex Your Resilience Muscles

Are there areas in your life where you have tried to skip the grief process? What will you do to allow yourself to grieve?

_____

_____

_____

_____

SELF-CARE

Taking care of yourself is another non-negotiable resilience-building strategy. I can't tell you how many times people told me to take care of myself, and my first thought was usually, "It would be great if I had time to do that, but I don't have the time!" It turns out the massage I got at the airport could have saved my life. The massage therapist is the one who originally found the tumor in my salivary gland.

Part of treating yourself well is to identify what recharges you. Make time to do these things. Whether it's a long soak in the tub, dinner with friends, or quiet time with a good book, give yourself some time to take care of you. Taking care of yourself means giving yourself permission to stop focusing on everyone else, and to start focusing on yourself. Treat yourself with kindness. So step back, breathe, give yourself a break, and take care of your number one resource: you.

My mom is a flight attendant, and she has fun with the in-flight announcements. My favorite is: "In case of a sudden loss of cabin pressure, please place your oxygen mask on first and then assist your child. If you have more than one child, pick your favorite, or the one with the most potential." We both share a somewhat warped sense of humor.

There is a very clear reason they ask adults to put their masks on first. If you aren't breathing, you won't be able to help anyone else. Whether it's a nap, a massage, a good book, or just sitting quietly, you must take time for yourself. The following sections are a few self-care strategies that have been hugely beneficial for me.

Mindfulness and Meditation

What are you thinking about right now? Your answer may provide some insight into your current level of resilience. A 2010 Harvard study found that people spend 47 percent of the time thinking about something other than what they are doing right now,[13] and I'm sure that number has grown since the study was conducted.

Technology and our current lifestyle have created a never-ending stream of information and stimulation. The constant distractions and chaos in our lives make it difficult to live in the moment. Our minds were not meant to be active 100 percent of the time. They need rest, quiet, and time to recharge. Meditation is basically a charging station for our brains. We charge our devices, and now it's time to charge ourselves. Meditation is a way to help calm and quiet the mind.

Andy Puddicombe, co-founder of the Headspace meditation app, says, "We are always busy in an attempt to create more time."[14] How true. We take time management classes, learn workflow processes, and make endless to-do lists, all in an attempt to find more time. Then, when we do have time, we fill it with things to try to make ourselves happy and content, only to feel more stressed and overwhelmed.

Puddicombe shares a straight-forward, three-step process:

Step 1: Have realistic expectations. Just because you "clear" your mind doesn't mean you won't still have random thoughts popping in and out. "What am I going to eat for dinner?" "I forgot to buy a present for the birthday party this weekend." "Why does my leg keep itching?" All kinds of thoughts will wander through your mind. It's normal. Expect it and let the thoughts roll on by, bringing yourself back to the present.

Step 2: Don't force it. It's like tossing and turning in the middle of the night, desperately trying to get to sleep faster so that you won't be tired in the morning. It just adds more anxiety. Instead of trying to force it, give yourself permission to just go with it, gently bringing yourself back. Keep breathing.

---

[13] Steve Bradt, "Wandering Mind Not a Happy Mind," *Harvard Gazette*, November 11, 2010, available at http://news.harvard.edu/gazette/story/2010/11/wandering-mind-not-a-happy-mind/.

[14] Andy Puddicombe, *Why Happiness Is Hard and How to Make It Easier*, SXSW Interactive 2016, March 15, 2016, available at https://www.youtube.com/watch?v=Iywlp4EbQf0.

Step 3: Let your thoughts pass by. Think of your thoughts like passing cars whizzing by on a highway. When you think about something, acknowledge it, and then watch it pass by. If you get stuck on a thought, don't try to force yourself to stop thinking about it. Just let it pass by at its own pace, and bring yourself back to taking deep breaths and being aware of your body.

UCLA, Harvard, Yale, and numerous other research programs have found that meditation literally changes the brain, and multiple studies show that it rivals the effectiveness of antidepressants for treating depression and anxiety.

What many once thought to be "fluff" has proven to be incredibly effective, even profitable. My insurance company instituted a mindfulness training program for employees. On average, stress levels dropped by almost 30 percent, sleep quality improved, and pain levels diminished. Participants gained an average of an hour of additional productivity each week, saving the company hundreds of thousands of dollars each year.[15]

We don't have to go on a week-long silent retreat to meditate, but we do have stop and be still. Our minds are used to running and being busy. Getting them to slow down will take some time and just like any other habit, meditation takes practice.

Jon Kabat-Zinn started a Mindfulness-Based Stress Reduction (MBSR) program, which he launched at the University of Massachusetts Medical School in 1979. Since then, thousands of studies have documented the physical and mental health benefits of mindfulness. Kabat-Zinn emphasizes that although mindfulness can be cultivated through formal meditation, that's not the only way. He explains, "It's not really about sitting in the full lotus, pretending you're a statue in a British museum. It's about living your life as if it really mattered, moment by moment."[16]

Some helpful ways to build mindfulness include paying attention to your breathing, identifying what you are feeling when you feel it,

---

[15] Theo Winter, *Evidence for Mindfulness: A Research Summary for the Corporate Sceptic*, March 25, 2016, available at www.td.org/Publications/Blogs/Science-of-Learning-Blog/2016/03/Evidence-for-Mindfulness.

[16] *What Is Mindfulness*, The Greater Good Science Center, available at http://greatergood.berkeley.edu/topic/mindfulness/definition.

noticing what is happening in your mind, and tapping into your body's physical senses. It requires you to simply be in the moment. Meditation and mindfulness can be used by anyone, anywhere, and they don't cost a thing.

Physical Exercise

I have suffered with depression from a young age. I was formally diagnosed when I was a freshman in college. Therapists used to tell me to exercise, sleep well, and take care of myself, and all I heard was, "blah blah blah." The last thing you want to do when you feel exhausted and sad is to exercise and eat a salad. It's much easier to lie around, binge watch TV, and eat food that's anything but good for you. Unfortunately, one begets the other, and you end up worse than you started.

Several years ago, I went through a particularly tough time. I started withdrawing, I wasn't sleeping well, and I was eating to numb my pain. My doctor suggested I exercise, eat right, and get enough sleep (shocking, I know).

We had moved into a neighborhood with a lap pool, and swimming was always the one exercise I didn't hate. I started out only swimming one or two laps, and I didn't notice feeling even the tiniest bit better. I kept at it, though, and after two or three weeks, I wanted to eat better because I noticed my body shape was changing. When I ate better, I lost weight, which made me want to swim more. The exercise made me tired, which provided the best sleep I'd had in years. In the course of six months, I lost 30 pounds and felt better than I could ever remember.

I still swim several times a week. I try to make healthy eating choices, and I make sleep a non-negotiable. It has been three years since my last relapse, and while I still get sad when we have difficult times with Evan, I don't sink into a hole. When I am stressed and anxious, swimming helps me calm down. It clears my mind.

Physical exercise is a key ingredient in building resilience, which has been proven to have positive effects on mood, improve the way we manage stress, and promote neurogenesis. Scientists have found that exercise helps the brain grow new neurons damaged by stress and can actually dampen your stress response, helping you to recover both physically and emotionally.

Find Reasons to Laugh

When we're stressed or tired, sometimes the idea of laughing and finding humor in situations seems impossible. This is all the more reason it is so important. Hell, laugh at yourself if you have to, but find ways to laugh.

The day after my eye surgery was my birthday. I was sporting a huge gauze bandage over my eye. And don't forget the giant boot on my broken foot. I was a sad sight.

Months before my birthday, Jay bought tickets for us to see Demetri Martin, one of my favorite comedians. I seriously debated whether or not to go to the show. Yes, it was my birthday, but I could not have felt any less festive if I tried. The last thing I wanted to do was go to dinner and a show. I was self-conscious enough.

As I said before, courage is not the absence of fear. It's being scared and doing it anyway. So we went to the show, and I laughed so hard my face hurt. Somehow, despite everything that had happened, I laughed.

Studies have revealed that a genuine smile (one that involves facial muscles around the eyes) sparks a change in brain activity related to a good mood. It slows down your heart rate during stress, causing you to relax. Laughter and humor really are the best medicine.

Flex Your Resilience Muscles

Can you name a time when you found humor in a delicate situation?

_____

_____

_____

_____

Continued on next page.

> **Flex Your Resilience Muscles** *Continued from the previous page.*
>
> What can you do to find humor in everyday situations?
>
> _____
>
> _____
>
> _____
>
> _____
>
> What can you do this week to find ways to laugh (listen to a comedian, read a funny book, etc.)?
>
> _____
>
> _____
>
> _____
>
> _____

Risk and Control

We can find resilience in all corners of our lives, including taking risks and relinquishing control. It is scary to risk failure, face your fears, and trust your gut. But it is also where resilience begins. Rather than risk failure, we play it safe, and that is a recipe for ripe and rotting.

Then comes the issue of control. What do you have control over, and how much time do you spend lamenting over things for which you have little or no control?

Here are a few examples of things you can directly control:

- How much time I spend worrying.
- How much money I spend.
- How often I pay it forward.
- How I compare myself to others.
- How physically active I am.
- How often I take risks.
- How often I tell the important people in my life that I love them.
- When and how I practice gratitude.
- How I manage stress.

- How I control my attitude and shift my paradigms for positive outcomes.
- How I take ownership of my life.
- How much negative self-talk I engage inside my head.

Flex Your Resilience Muscles

Where could you take a calculated risk? It would be great if I could...

_____

_____

_____

_____

Sample answers might include:
- Learn a new language.
- Learn to dance the Salsa.
- Build my own business.
- De-clutter my home.

What risk can you take this week to get out of your comfort zone?

_____

_____

_____

_____

What can you add to the list of things you can directly control?

_____

_____

_____

_____

"Out of your vulnerabilities will come your strength."

—Sigmund Freud

Seek and You Will Find

We find what we look for. It's as simple as that. Think back to someone that you dated, that at the time, you thought could be "the one." At first, everything this person did was magical. The way they talked was adorable. The way they laughed made you smile. At some point, when you figured out they were indeed not "the one," everything they did made you crazy. You got disgusted listening to them chew. Watching them eat made you nauseated. How did everything change?

Think about the last time you bought a car. Chances are, once you started thinking about a specific car, you started to notice it all over the place. Last year, we took a family road trip and rented an RV. There is nothing better than getting to bond with family in a small, confined space. It was the first time we had rented an RV, and it was in every way like the movie with Robin Williams. The fascinating thing was that we started to see RVs everywhere. It's like they were taking over the roads. I had never really paid attention before, and I had never really seen them.

You find what you look for. The problem is that when you look for the negative, you find it in spades. It is easy to slip down a negative spiral. Training your brain to look for the good things is a process and requires patience and practice. Building courage and resilience requires you to look for the right things.

Do What Works for You

There are many additional ways to build resilience. Volunteering for a meaningful cause, facing your fears, having a strong set of values and beliefs, surrounding yourself with positive people, and being optimistic are just a few examples.

Specifically, optimism is the inclination to adopt the most hopeful interpretation of any event. It's a trait that influences your emotions and is associated with greater resilience. Begin to focus your intentions on the most positive interpretations of the situation, and you will be surprised at how much more optimistic you feel.

Generosity has also proven to be a highly successful way to build resilience. Being generous with your financial resources is great, but research has found that doing things for others and volunteering your time are most likely to cultivate happiness and resilience.

The key is to find what works for you and do more of it.

Flex Your Resilience Muscles

Which of the resilience strategies listed above will you try?

_____

_____

_____

_____

HANDLING RESILIENCY SLUMPS

There will be times when you go through periods in which you have low energy, feel discouraged, or struggle with your life, job, relationships, etc.

Make a deliberate effort to do things on purpose that help you recover your energy level. Even if you don't feel like it. *Especially* if you don't feel like it. Whatever you do, don't give yourself a hard time for hitting a slump period. The key is to keep moving.

A few things to remember:

- Don't compare yourself to others.
- Stop trying to fix people. All you can do is shift your behavior.
- Forgive…yourself and others. Let go of anger and resentment.
- Stop waiting for permission. This is your life, and you have to own it.

Flex Your Resilience Muscles

What can you do right now to build resilience?

_____

_____

_____

_____

WHEN RESILIENCE BECOMES A STROKE OF INSIGHT AND COURAGE

I have written and spoken on the subject of emotional intelligence and emotional resilience for years. Perhaps because of Evan's struggles I have a very special perspective on resilience, along with great respect and fondness for the brain and its enormous capacity to give us strength, soft and hard skill sets, intuition, well-being, and so much more.

By understanding basic parts of the brain—even a wounded brain—we can repair broken minds and even hearts, and recalibrate our resilience to find greater courage and rebound with extraordinary abilities and insights we may never before have imagined.

For one young woman, it all came down to a "stroke of insight." One of the most amazing examples of human resilience and the brain's ability to recover from the most traumatic and agonizing of circumstances is the story of Dr. Jill Bolte Taylor.[17]

Taylor is no stranger to NAMI. She is passionate about the work NAMI does. Her brother suffers from schizophrenia, and Taylor devoted her entire career to brain science so that she could better understand what was happening to her brother and to their family.

---

[17] Jill Bolte Taylor, *My Stroke of Insight: A Brain Scientist's Personal Journey* (London: Penguin Books, 2008).

The Explosion

One December morning in Cambridge, Massachusetts, Taylor woke up with a pounding pain behind her left eye. She made herself get up and get ready for work despite the agony she felt, not knowing she was having a massive stroke. A brain scientist at Harvard University, Taylor was only 37 years old at the time.

There are many different kinds of strokes from which people suffer—some mild and easy to recover from and others that bring them to their knees or even kill them. Unfortunately, Taylor experienced the worst kind of stroke imaginable. A blood vessel literally exploded in her brain. Within the course of four hours, alone in her apartment, she lost her ability to talk, read, write, or recall any of her life. She literally became an infant inside a woman's body.

The Power of the Brain

Our brains have both the capacity for being linear and methodical, as well as creative and intuitive. When we talk about a person's intellect, we sometimes refer to a person's intelligence quotient (IQ) or their logical way of thinking. When we talk about emotional intelligence (EQ or EI), we are often referring to the part of the brain where so many of the creative and soft skills of reasoning, patience, getting along with others, and sensitive feelings reside.

The beauty of knowing more about your brain is also knowing that you have the power to activate both parts and make the most out of your circumstances—I call this emotional resilience.

Taylor's experience is a phenomenal example of the power we have to activate either part of the brain to help us be all that we can be and even survive a devastating occurrence, just like she did.

During the stroke, Taylor alternated between two realities—one a beautiful nirvana of consciousness, simply wanting to let go and be free; the other aware of the grave situation that repeatedly told her to "Get help! Now!"

With what little consciousness she had remaining, Taylor activated and called upon called upon her creative brain to figure out how to match the phone number on her business card with the numbers on the telephone that she could no longer read. It took her 45 minutes to punch in the numbers to her office, and when her colleague answered the telephone, all she heard was "Arggh arggh, arggh," like the adults talking in a Charlie Brown movie. And on the other end of the line, all her colleague heard from Taylor was, "Arggh, arggh, arggh," because she had lost the ability to speak. Her office called for help and an ambulance was sent to her apartment.

Recovery through Resilience

Taylor teaches us that we can use both the logical and creative parts of our brains to find and practice courage and resilience.

Taylor's story is one of both physically and emotionally stirring recovery. It's a story of resilience at its highest level. Over a period of eight years, she recovered fully with the help of her mother, who recently passed away. Taylor continues to speak prophetically and passionately to audiences worldwide about the resilient mind and all of the insights to be gained by understanding the brain, and the power we have to activate the parts that we need the most during times when we are desperately seeking inner strength and courage.

The most amazing things in life tend to happen right at the moment you're about to let go and give up. Your thoughts drive your actions. Your actions become your habits. Resilience is a habit.

"Being defeated is often a temporary condition. Giving up is what makes it permanent." —Marilyn vos Savant

Flex Your Resilience Muscles

Think about a time you were knocked down emotionally and you did not necessarily recover as quickly as you would have liked. Describe that time here.

_____

_____

_____

_____

_____

_____

_____

Now think about an instance in which you did rebound and recover quickly. How do these two examples compare? What made it possible to bounce back? When you examine the differences you can start closing the gaps.

_____

_____

_____

_____

_____

_____

_____

WHAT NOW?

Think of things that make you feel strong and inspired. Do these things intentionally and often. If listening to music inspires you, then play your favorite tunes and turn up the volume. Listen to the music until you can actually *hear* it again. In fact, we can often associate a song with a feeling. When we hear the song, dopamine (the feel-good neurotransmitter) is released in our brains, making us actually feel happier. What song does that for you?

The key is to make a conscious decision to exercise resilience. Here are just a few examples of ways to do that:

- Refuse to get overly upset by the little things.
- Forgive yourself for mistakes, both little and big.
- Remain calm when someone treats you disrespectfully.
- Manage stress proactively before an important event.

"Life doesn't get easier or more forgiving; we get stronger and more resilient." —Dr. Steve Maraboli

Flex Your Resilience Muscles

Is there anything holding you back at this point in your life? What are the barriers?

_____

_____

_____

_____

How will you step out of your comfort zone to build resilience?

_____

_____

_____

_____

PART 3:
TRIUMPH

PART 3:
TRIUMPH

Over the course of the past year while writing this book, I have sought out and had conversations with people all over the world about their courage and resilience. I have read hundreds of articles; completed two TEDx talks; and been interviewed by and spoken with top-notch leaders, innovators, aspiring entrepreneurs, and spiritual gurus.

I've asked people time and again how they stay strong enough to face daily challenges, heartbreak, tears, and disappointment. The answers were as varied as the people I asked, but one common theme emerged: choice. Failure was not an option for these people. They chose courage over fear, they chose resilience over defeat, and they chose to triumph despite adversity because they believed there was no other choice.

FROM HEARTACHE TO TRIUMPH—IT'S A TRAPEZE ACT

A woman I met told me that she is very visual and keeps a picture on the night stand in her bedroom of a couple on a trapeze. (I thought, "Whoa, lady, this may be more than I need to know." But she quickly explained herself.)

In the photo, the couple is swinging high above the ground. It's clear that the woman is getting ready to let go and grab onto her partner's outstretched hands. She told me this symbolizes everything she's tried to let go of in her life, including the trust she's been so desperate to feel toward others, and the freedom to gain peace of mind that she needs to embrace—all of this so that she can triumph in the here and now.

What a great way to look at things. You can't become the person you were meant to be without letting go of where you have been. Setbacks and tragedies are horrible, but they do not have to define us.

I love the idea of a visual like this. It really helps when trying to form a new habit to have a visual reminder. For this lady, it was the trapeze artists, but it can be anything.

You can only find your courage when you start behaving courageously. Just like the couple on the trapeze, letting go requires courage, trust, and lots of patience and practice. If you want to be a better swimmer, you swim. If you want to be a better musician, you play more music. And when I wanted to become a better speaker, I gave tons of speeches, hired a coach, and developed new content, connected with speaker bureaus, and wrote my second book. Then, I practiced over and over and over. I let go of my old ways of doing things and started grabbing on to new and improved ways of doing things...things that would push me to be bigger, bolder, and braver. And make no mistake about it, all of those things were uncomfortable. Unfortunately, if you don't take risks and do things differently, you will end up with the same results.

This doesn't happen overnight. I had to find my courage. I had to let go of the old stuff that wasn't working for me. And I'm still learning to let go and will hopefully keep doing so for the rest of my life.

Letting go is a positive act. It's not necessarily negative and it doesn't represent loss. When we let go, what we are really doing is "connecting" and "gaining" greater options in life. But you must let go of something to grab on to something else bigger and better, even when it's uncomfortable.

Even when you are reaching for new experiences, positive choices, and a better future, letting go is still scary. Courage means you do it anyway.

Flex Your Triumph Muscles

- **Create a visual.** What images come to mind when you think of triumph?
- **Make a connection.** Connect the symbolic nature of the visual to your own struggles and fears. This helps you to connect to the picture physically, mentally, emotionally, intellectually, consciously, and subconsciously.
- **Visualize letting go.** Intentionally visualize yourself letting go of people, things, regrets, shame, blame, imperfections, and anything else that keeps you stuck.
- **Out of sight, out of mind.** Put it somewhere you will see it every day.

"Learn to let go. That is the key to happiness." —Buddha

TRIUMPH IS GAINING THE ABILITY TO CONNECT AND BE VULNERABLE

When we quit worrying about what other people think, we become disconnected and cold. When we let other people define us, we lose ourselves. Connecting and being vulnerable is a delicate balance. It means listening to constructive feedback and viewing it objectively. It means taking risks and trying new things, even if it is scary, and it means allowing yourself to be vulnerable.

Discovering triumph really is like swinging from a trapeze high above the ground, having the focus and discipline to let go because we have a safety net of people who truly care about us and want us to succeed.

CHOOSE YOUR EXPECTATIONS WISELY

Ray Wylie Hubbard is a great Texas singer and songwriter. One of his lyrics sums it up perfectly. He sings, "And the days that I keep my gratitude higher than my expectations, well, I have really good days." I have found that when I'm unhappy, frustrated, sad, or disappointed, it is usually because my expectations and reality are out of alignment. We can't always control what makes up our reality, but we can certainly choose our expectations.

We all have expectations of how we think people *should be* and *should behave.* So much unnecessary heartache arises in relationships when people fail to act in accordance with our standards and expectations. Unmet expectations are a great way to build hurt, anger, and resentment.

In social psychology, the fundamental attribution error refers to our tendency to judge others by their behavior and assign it to their character, but to judge ourselves by our intent. Essentially, we blame. We make assumptions about people's motives. When they exhibit a behavior we don't like, we label it as a character flaw. For example, you see someone run a stop sign. You may think, "Jerk! Where are the cops when you need them? You could have killed someone!" But when you accidentally run a stop sign, you think, "Oops. I was distracted. I'm so glad the cops weren't here and that no one got hurt."

Think of the last time you were on a plane, in a restaurant, or somewhere else where a baby was screaming. It is so easy in that situation to judge the parents—until you are one of them. Once when Evan was little, a man literally threw Tootsie Rolls at us down several rows on a plane just to get Evan to stop crying. Like I hadn't already tried that. If all it took to calm him down was some candy, I would have dated Willy Wonka! I remember feeling mortified and embarrassed.

My life got a whole lot easier when I started giving people the benefit of the doubt. I don't think most people wake up thinking, "How many people can I disappoint today?" I genuinely believe that most of us are doing the best we can with what we have. If you were to pull the roof tops off all our homes, you would see that we are all dealing with something. We are all doing the best we can, and we have to give each other a break and the benefit of the doubt.

Then there are our expectations of ourselves. I am what Brené Brown would call a "recovering perfectionist" or an "aspiring good enoughist." I've been a perfectionist since I was a little girl. Recently, my mom reminded me that I refused to eat until I could learn how to tie my own shoes…when I was two. It's hard to be strong when you never know if it is strong enough.

The only way to beat perfectionism is to acknowledge where we are most vulnerable. We all go through the universal experiences of shame, judgment, blame, lack of self-esteem, and even self-loathing. It is only through our willingness to embrace our imperfections—no, make that love and appreciate our imperfections—that we can find courage, emotional intelligence, resilience, compassion for one another, and that ever-so-elusive peace of mind.

"The thing that is really hard, and really amazing is giving up on being perfect and beginning the work of becoming yourself." —Anna Quindlen

ACCEPTANCE IS A LIFE LESSON

I'm sure you've experienced let downs and disappointments. In fact, you may even have people in your life right now who upset you with what they do or don't do.

The fact is, like it or not, you have to accept other people's behavior (it's theirs, not yours). Stop expecting others to be something they are not, including attempts to make them be the way you imagine them being, or the way you think they should be. People are not projects. It's the only way to stop your own suffering and disappointment. It's hard enough to change your own behavior, let alone believe you have the power to change someone else's. When you shift your expectations, life gets a whole lot easier.

"Accept people for who they are, not who you want them to be." —Anonymous

Acceptance Doesn't Mean Compromising Your Values

I want to be perfectly clear about something. Accepting other people for who they are does not mean that you have to condone or tolerate behavior you think is wrong. If someone is drinking and driving, hurting a child, stealing, or being a bigot, you'd say, "No way! That's not what I stand for. You'll have to live your life without me in your inner circle. If you need help to recover, get therapy, or if you want support to improve your life, then I'm right here. But I won't condone or tolerate wrong doing. Period." Being courageous and resilient requires clear boundaries and unwavering values.

Acceptance Applies to the Workplace, Too

We can only leverage inclusion, diversity, cultural competency, and tolerance in the workplace if we value people's unique differences and accept who and what people are, for what they are.

A superstar team is one that complements and supports each member. Our open hearts and open minds turbo-charge the workplace and enhance productivity, great service, and performance.

The next time you're at a retreat or in a meeting and someone comes up with something totally off the wall, before you laugh, mentally blow them off, or make a statement you may regret, ask yourself how the team might benefit from the unique approach and person's style. Are there any strengths you can find in this approach? Is it worth a try? This is a good time to use judgment, not pass judgment.

Flex Your Triumph Muscles

When was the last time you judged someone according to their behavior? What would you have done differently if you had given them the benefit of the doubt and assumed positive intent?

_____

_____

_____

_____

Has anyone ever misread your intent? When was the last time you did something and someone passed judgment that made you feel embarrassed or ashamed?

_____

_____

_____

_____

A WORK IN PROGRESS

I wish I could say that I have matured to the point where I never get hurt when people don't act the way I wish they would. The truth is I still get hurt. I slip up. But I'm making progress as I honor my inner courage, resilience, and the desire to triumph in my personal and professional life.

Getting the hang of all of this takes time. It doesn't happen overnight. We are all works-in-progress and learning to let go happens gradually. I try every single day to be a better person and to let go of my expectations of others and grab on to them (like in the trapeze photograph) fully for who they are and where they are in their lives right now.

RELINQUISH CONTROL

As a self-professed control freak, I find this next sentence extremely hard to remember, but it's absolutely necessary to triumph. You are *not in* control, nor will you ever be. The longer you try to hang on to the myth that you can control everything, the more limitations you will put on all the possibilities that lay before you. However, when you let go, you automatically create more strength in your body and your mind, you grow your emotional intelligence to take risks, and you begin to savor this thing we call life and all of its rich and tangy experiences. But most of all, you will have finally let go of who you thought you were supposed to be and embrace the real you.

On an average day at my house, I dole out dozens of orders and requests: "Take your dishes in the kitchen and rinse them." "Walk the dogs." "Take out the trash." "Make your lunch." "Call the plumber." "Pick up bread." I have often thought, "How would this house survive if I weren't here to make sure everything gets done?!"

But guess what? When I had my surgery and wasn't able to do anything, or when I'm traveling for work, things miraculously get done. The sky doesn't fall, life continues, and everything is okay. It's a hard lesson to learn. We are NOT in control.

Flex Your Triumph Muscles

What do you try to control in your life? How can you begin to relinquish control?

_____

_____

_____

_____

_____

_____

PRACTICE INTEGRITY

Brené Brown says that integrity means "You choose courage over comfort. You choose what is right over what is fun, fast, or easy. And you choose to practice your values rather than simply professing them."[18] Being triumphant means that you are true to yourself, that you live from a place of integrity. This isn't always easy. Sometimes it means speaking up when it would be easier to remain silent. And sometimes it means staying silent when you really want to speak up.

"Courage is what it takes to stand up and speak; courage is also what it takes to sit down and listen." —Winston Churchill

FIND PEACE AMONG THE MADNESS

Inertia can be your greatest friend or worst enemy. After reading this book, you have a choice: You can take what you have learned and embark on a courage and resilience journey, or you can stay with your comfortable habits. Although I know it is much easier to stay comfortable, I'd like to challenge you to pick one strategy and take action. Then, take another, and another. Movement and momentum—without them we stay stuck.

Here is what I do know for sure. We—meaning every single one of us—have to get up every day and take at least one baby step. We move toward being the best we can be, forgiving ourselves for our shortcomings, and appreciating all of the parts that make us who we are. We move toward digging deeper to find our courage, build our resilience, and triumph over the obstacles life throws our way.

Move toward calm and stillness when you can. Be mindful of how you are feeling and thinking. Let go of working so hard to be the person you think others expect you to be. Become okay with who you are today, and forgive yourself when you slip up.

---

[18] Brené Brown, *Rising Strong: The Reckoning, the Rumble, the Revolution* (New York: Spiegal & Grau, 2015).

THE END OF THIS BOOK
STARTS WITH YOUR GRATITUDE QUEST

Author Melody Beattie explains that gratitude unlocks the fullness of life.[19] It turns what we have into enough, and more. It turns denial into acceptance, chaos to order, and confusion to clarity. It can turn a meal into a feast, a house into a home, a stranger into a friend. Gratitude makes sense of our past, brings peace for today, and creates a vision for tomorrow.

"Gratitude makes sense of our past, brings peace for today and creates a vision for tomorrow." —Melody Beattie

HAPPINESS COMES FROM GRATITUDE

The rate of suicide, depression, and self-medication are higher in the Western world than any other place on Earth. We appear prosperous on the outside, but on the inside we are emotionally starving. We've somehow adopted the notion that we can purchase happiness and even more…a perfect life.

In reality, the more we seek perfection and the less time we spend embracing and being grateful for our imperfections, the more deeply depressed and dissatisfied we become.

Attitude isn't enough. People often say if you have the right attitude, you automatically get gratitude. I disagree.

From the seeds of attitude come a basis for great understanding and acceptance. But from the seeds of vulnerability and joy, come gratitude.

When we are fearful, all we get is more scarcity and less joy. We start contemplating that maybe the happiness we're experiencing won't last and is fleeting. We fear that if we give in to feelings of happiness and joyfulness, we will eventually be inviting disaster, or worse, we may believe that we really don't *deserve* to be happy anyway. Then, up come our inadequacies and imperfections, staring us right in the face.

---

[19] Melody Beattie, *Journey to the Heart: Daily Meditations on the Path to Freeing Your Soul* (San Francisco: Harper, 1996).

When you are taken over by despair and sadness, you diminish your ability to be resilient and strong. Allow joy and gratitude to come into your heart. None of us can prepare for bad times before they happen. I could never have prepared myself for being the mother of a mentally ill child. But I know that today, I am stronger and better for all I have been through as a result.

GRATITUDE DOESN'T ALWAYS COME EASILY

How are you supposed to feel grateful when you just lost your job, your child is ill, or you just suffered a broken heart? Sure, it's easy to be grateful when you have money in the bank, the bills are paid, your family is healthy, and you just got a promotion at work. But what about when that's not the case?

Gratitude is not measured by how you are feeling during the worst of times; rather, it involves acknowledging that something good still exists for you. It's a rare and unique form of courtesy to oneself.

"Gratitude is the most exquisite form of courtesy."

—Jacques Maritain

Dr. Robert Emmons, a psychologist at University of California, Davis, describes gratitude as involving two stages.[20] The first is acknowledging what is good in your life. The second is recognizing that the source of these good things lies at least partially outside of yourself.

Emmons found that gratitude helps people feel more positive emotions, relish good experiences, improve their health, deal with adversity, and build strong relationships. Gratitude has additional benefits, and what's interesting is that you don't have to find anything to be grateful for. You just have to look. The simple act of looking releases serotonin and dopamine, the feel good neurotransmitters in your brain.[21]

---

[20] Robert Emmons, Why Gratitude Is Good, The Greater Good Science Center, available at http://greatergood. berkeley.edu/article/item/why_gratitude_is_good.

[21] Alex Korb and Daniel J. Siegel, *The Upward Spiral: Using Neuroscience to Reverse the Course of Depression, One Small Change at a Time* (Oakland, CA: New Harbinger Publications, 2015).

Flex Your Triumph Muscles

List three things that have happened today for which you feel grateful.

_____

_____

_____

_____

What can you do each day to remind yourself to focus on gratitude?

_____

_____

_____

_____

"Gratitude is not only the greatest of virtues, but the parent of all the others." —Marcus Tullius Cicero

MAKING IT STICK

Behavior change is difficult. You increase your odds of success exponentially by creating a plan of action to use what you have learned. Take a moment to record your best ideas for each section. Then, create a plan of action to apply what you have learned.

Flex Your Triumph Muscles

Record your best ideas from each section.

Courage

_____

_____

_____

_____

Resilience

_____

_____

_____

_____

Triumph

_____

_____

_____

_____

How will you apply what you have learned?

_____

_____

_____

_____

COURAGE + RESILIENCE = TRIUMPH

Conclusion

I wrote this book because I have learned firsthand what it takes to find courage, how to grow resilience, and appreciate moments of triumph. By sharing some of my experiences, many others have felt comfortable doing the same. And from their stories I have learned the true meaning of courage, worthiness, and hard-core resilience. In the end, it has all been a gift. Through the pain and sorrow and sometimes pitch darkness, I have become more grateful than I ever could have imagined.

As you embark on your journey, remember to celebrate your courage and resilience and savor the little moments of triumph. Never take what you have for granted. Cherish it. And never, ever apologize for your good fortune. All you have to do is be grateful and share your gratitude with those around you. Pay it forward. And while you're at it, tell people how much they mean to you. Don't wait for a special occasion. Do it today. We never know what tomorrow will bring.

And if someone you know has suffered great loss, be compassionate and listen. It is not a call to diminish what you have. If you have a friend who is struggling, offer your support, but be grateful for what is good in your life. Never shrink yourself because of the sadness around you. Just the opposite—grow your ability to love and be loved.

And finally, know that real happiness and satisfaction comes to us often in mundane moments that are ordinary, not extraordinary. If you are chasing all the big moments in life, you are much more likely to miss out on the small, simple sunsets on the beach, or the laughter of a child playing. Happiness doesn't always come from the big things. Pay attention to the little smiles, laugher, and joy.

It is my sincere hope that within these pages you have found your inner voice of courage; a greater, stronger, emotional resilience; and your most triumphant spirit. Whatever was is now in the past, but tomorrow is yet to be realized. You control your life and your destiny. This is just the beginning. Enjoy the journey!

And remember: Get off your ass and be grateful!

"We do not need a magic wand to transform from fear to triumph. We have all the power we require inside ourselves, at this very moment." —Anne Grady

ABOUT THE AUTHOR

*S*peaker, author, and cake lover Anne Grady inspires audiences around the world, providing practical strategies that can be applied both personally and professionally to improve relationships, navigate change, and overcome adversity. With her signature style of wit and candor, Anne helps people muster their courage, find their resilience, and claim their triumph.

Anne holds a master's degree in Organizational Communication. She lives in Round Rock, Texas, with her husband, two children, and their "therapy" dogs Bernie and Charlie.

For details on how to bring the strategies in this book into your conference or organization, or to learn about the other organizational development solutions available, contact Anne at (512) 821-1111 or email her at hello@annegradygroup.com. You can also visit her online at www.annegradygroup.com.

Keep in touch and share your success stories with Anne!

 Facebook.com/AnneGradyGroup

 YouTube.com/AnneGradyGroup

 Twitter.com/AnneGradyGroup

 Instagram.com/AnneGradyGroup

 www.annegradygroup.com/blog